105 Things God Says About You...

Appropriating Your Inheritance

105 Things God says About You...

Appropriating Your Inheritance

2nd Edition

E. C. Nakeli

King's Word Publishing

© 2018 by E.C. Nakeli

Published by King's Word Publication

2nd edition

For your questions and publishing needs, write to:

    CMFI
    40 S Church st
    Westminster, MD 21157
    E-mail: *ecnakeli@yahoo.com*

Printed in the United States of America

All rights reserved. No part of this publication may be reproduced, stored in a retrieval systems, or transmitted in ay form or by any means—for example, electronic, photocopy, recording—without the prior written permission of the publisher. The only exception is brief quotations in printed reviews.

E.C. Nakeli

To contact the author, write to:

    E.C. Nakeli
    40 S Church st
    Westminster, MD 21157
    E-mail: *ecnakeli@yahoo.com*

105 Things God Says About You... Appropriating Your Inheritance/ E.C. Nakeli

ISBN: 9781945055171

    Unless otherwise indicated, Scriptures references are from
    THE HOLY BIBLE, NEW INTERNATIONAL VERSION®, NIV®
    Copyright © 1973, 1978, 1984, 2011 by Biblica, Inc™
    Used by permission. All rights reserved worlwide.

Cover and Interior Design: Zach Essama

Table of Contents

Preface to Second Edition 1
Introduction 3

#1: You are the salt of the earth 5
#2: You are the light of the world 7
#3: You have the knowledge of the secrets of the kingdom 9
#4: Everything is yours for teh asking 11
#5: You have authority to bind and loose 13
#6: You have the genes of God in you 15
#7: You are secure in Christ 17
#8: You have a prepared and guaranteed place in heaven 19
#9: You are spiritually clean 21
#10: You are a branch of the Vine 23
#11: You were specially chosen by the Lord 25
#12: You do not belong to the world 27
#13: You are entitled to the Holy Ghost baptism 29
#14: Your period and place of living was pre-determined by God 31
#15: You live and move and have your being in God 33
#16: You have been freed from sin 35
#17: You are free from condemnation 37
#18: You are Controlled by the Spirit 39
#19: Your present suffering cannot compare to the glory awaiting you 41
#20: All of creation is awaiting your manifestation 43
#21: The Spirit intercedes for you 45
#22: All things work together for your good 47
#23: Because God is for you, it doesn't matter who is against you 49
#24: Nothing can separate you from God's love 51

#25: Christ has become your righteousness and holiness 53
#26: You have been washed, sanctified and justified................................55
#27: Your body is God's temple 57
#28: You have been anointed and sealed by God 59
#29: Christ died for you so that you may live for Him 61
#30: You are a new creature in Christ 63
#31: You are Christ's ambassador 65
#32: You are blessed 67
#33: You are Abraham's seed...69
#34: You have every spiritual blessing you need 71
#35: You are seated with Christ in the heavenly places.........................73
#36: You are a citizen of heaven..75
#37: God who started His work in you will bring it to completion..........77
#38: You have been qualified to share in the inheritance of the saints 79
#39: God has brought you into the Kingdom of Christ........................81
#40: You are holy and dearly loved 83
#41: God will strengthen and protect you 85
#42: You have the Spirit of power, love, and boldness..........................87
#43: You are a royal priest..89
#44: You have everything you need for life and godliness 91
#45: You have overcome the evil one 93
#46: You are a child of God...95
#47: God is able to keep you from falling..97
#48: God gives you everything for your enjoyment 99
#49: God has assigned your portion 101
#50: God will guide you always...103
#51: God loads each day with benefits for you 105
#52: Your past sins have been separated far from you.........................107
#53: God will keep you from all harm...109
#54: God knew you before you were born..111
#55: You are God's special handiwork 113
#56: God's thoughts about you are numerous and precious..................115

#57: God has good plans for you 117
#58: God will never leave you nor abandon you till you fulfil your destiny.. 119
#59: No weapon formed against you shall prosper................................121
#60: No witchcraft can work against you...123
#61: All who attack you will surrender to you 125
#62: God will give men in exchange for you...127
#63: God will make your rough places smooth......................................129
#64: He will give you the treasures of darkness 131
#65: What God has planned for you, nothing can thwart....................133
#66: It is your season to shine...135
#67: You are a fortified city..137
#68: You are an iron pillar 139
#69: You are a god..141
#70: You are the apple of God's eye 143
#71: You are engraved on the palms of God's hands 145
#72: You are a spiritual Imperialist 147
#73: You are a terror to the devil 149
#74: You are surrounded with favour..151
#75: You are more than a conqueror..153
#76: You can love everybody 155
#77: You have overcome the world 157
#78: You have been healed...159
#79: You are a child of promise 161
#81: You were made in the image of God..165
#82: You were fashioned to be in control...167
#83: You are a child of destiny..169
#84: God has made you storm and flame resistant..............................171
#85: You are God's treasured possession...173
#86: Your future is brighter than your present 175
#87: Goodness and mercy have been assigned to you 177
#88: You have the power to shape your destiny....................................179

#89: There are angels all around you 181
#90: You are a living flame of fire 183
#91: You are an heir of the Father 185
#92: You have resurrection power in you 187
#93: There are rivers flowing inside of you 189
#94: Everything is possible for you if you believe 191
#95: God has made you invincible 193
#96: You have divine immunity 195
#97: Your deliverance is guaranteed 197
#98: You should always be at the top 199
#99: God knows what you need 201
#100: You are useless without Christ Jesus 203
#101: It shall be well with you 205
#102: You will enjoy the fruit of your labour 207
#103: Your life is hidden with Christ in God 209
#104: You are married to Christ 211
#105: God will give you singleness of heart 213

Conclusion 215

Preface to Second Edition

This is the second and revised edition of *"105 Things God Says About You"*, first published in 2010. I have revised and expanded most of the points shared in the first edition to bring more clarity. There is tremendous power released in the spoken word. What a man hears will greatly influence his conduct or behaviour, appearance and performance. There are many lives which are being destroyed because people have tried to build their lives on what others have said about them. They react according to what the world says about them, and unconsciously become moulded into the cast of human opinion. It doesn't matter the label your enemies, friends, family, colleagues, peers or whoever has given you. If you know what God says about you, then you can live life with your head lifted high irrespective of the cynics, sceptics and critiques.

The apostle Paul told Timothy in 1Timothy 1:18 to follow the prophecies that were once made about him. This book just brings out some prophecies God has given to his children, so, believe and follow them. In so doing you will be moulding your life in the cast of the Divine will.

INTRODUCTION

Whatever knowledge a man possesses greatly influences what he does and how he reacts to people and situations. Ignorance is the lack of useful knowledge and acts as a great limitation to the extent of exploits its victim can carry. I have often said that ignorance is one of the great diseases which have plagued humankind and there is continuously a great need to eradicate this ill especially among the saints.

The Lord God said, *"My people are destroyed from lack of knowledge"* (Hosea 4:6a). Hence, it is neither the power of your enemy which is destroying you nor his wisdom but your lack of heart or spiritual knowledge which is the problem. Why do I say heart knowledge? Because spiritual matters are matters of the heart and not the head! There are many people with a lot of head knowledge but until it is conveyed to the heart it produces very little results. Thus, the purpose of this little book is not to swell your head but to expand your heart and bring you to a position where the output of your life is influenced by what you know.

It should be noted that what I am about sharing in this book are what God says concerning His children, those who have made an irreversible commitment to obey the Lord Jesus Christ. It would not do you any good to just pick up this book and read it through. You may claim everything outlined here but it will not work for you until you come into that vital and unconditional surrender to Jesus Christ as your personal Lord and Saviour. Do not hesitate to pray this prayer if you want the Lord Jesus to come into your heart right now so that you can benefit from all what will be said here. If you are ready then just pray like this, with all sincerity:

"Lord Jesus, I admit that I am a sinner. I admit that You died for me. I come to You this moment with all my sins; past present

and future. I ask for Your forgiveness. Wash me with your blood and cleans me from all my sins. Give me a new heart and a new spirit. Help me to love You and to serve You all the days of my life. Take my heart and make it your home. Amen"

If you sincerely prayed that prayer then you are now fit to claim all that will be shared in here. May God bless you as you read and believe His word, and may He bring you into all what He has ordained for you!

#1

YOU ARE THE SALT OF THE EARTH

(Matthew 5:13)

"You are the salt of the earth. But if the salt loses its saltiness, how can it be made salty again? It is no longer good for anything, except to be thrown out and trampled by men."

Because you are the salt of the earth, this means you are a preservative. You have the capacity to prevent moral and spiritual decay wherever you are. Just like salt prevents microbes from functioning and causing decay, you have the inherent capacity to hinder the devil's actions wherever you are. Your presence in your family should keep things from decaying there. Your presence in that place of work should hinder the devil and his human agents from functioning in the fulness of their capacity, and why not put a total stop to their activities? You are earth's preservative!

Also, salt provides taste. Things should get sweeter because of your presence. The day you leave that office or work place, things will no longer be as sweet as when you were there. God made it that way and the devil cannot deny it. He may get angry, but he knows the God's children are those preserving this earth and giving it the taste, it deserves. The day we will be taken away, everything will turn bitter and rot at the speed of light. Leave your home daily and tell yourself you are going out to prevent decay and provide heavenly taste everywhere you go.

Proclaim what you are

Father, I thank you for what You say concerning me. I believe Your word with all my heart and. with all my soul. I refuse to believe what my circumstances say. I refuse to believe what people say I stand on your word and therefore confess that I am what You say I am. And I am who You say I am.

I am the salt of the earth. I have not lost my saltiness. I will not lose my saltiness. I will preserve things from decaying around me. I will provide the taste required in a tasteless world. I will not be contaminated but will keep myself pure. In Jesus' awesome Name, amen.

# #
2

YOU ARE THE LIGHT OF THE WORLD

(Matthew 5:14; Ephesians 5:8)

"You are the light of the world. A city on a hill cannot be hidden."
"For you were once darkness, but now you are light in the Lord.
Live as children of light"

Light is what causes people to see and therefore function normally. The Lord said you are the light of the world. This means that your words and actions will either shine that light unto the right path or unto the wrong path. When you do the right things, you point your light for people to choose the right path. Without you darkness will cover the world and things will fly apart. It is the ignorance of the world that makes them hate God's children.

Your presence in that office or neighbourhood provides light and dispels the darkness that will otherwise cover that place. Decide that you will shine your light unto the path of life for others to see the way and follow. Keep yourself in contact with the source of power so that your light will continue to shine. Many people's light gets put off because they bridge vital contact with the power house. Keep vital fellowship with the True Vine and live conscious of the shining light you carry.

Step into every place with the intention to let your light shine. Sometimes, when you get into a place, as your light shines those who love the darkness may react negatively towards you, not because of anything you said or did, but because they are uncomfortable with the light you have brought. Some reactions toward you is not about you but about the light you carry.

Proclaim what you are

Father, I thank you for what You say concerning me. I believe Your word with all my heart and with all my soul. I refuse to believe what my circumstances say. I refuse to believe what people say. I stand on your word and therefore confess that I am what You say I am. And I am who You say I am.

I am the light of the world. My light cannot be put out. I will let my light shine where you have placed me and in what you have given me to do. I will shine the light of my life on the path of life so others can find The Way. Darkness cannot stand my presence. I will dispel darkness wherever I go and in whatever I do. I will maintain vital contact with the source of power so as to shine the brightest possible, in Jesus' mighty Name, amen.

#3

YOU HAVE THE KNOWLEDGE OF THE SECRETS OF THE KINGDOM

(Matthew 13:11)

"The knowledge of the secrets of the kingdom of heaven has been given to you, but not to them."

The kingdom of God has secrets which lead you to enjoy the abundance that is hidden there within. You know treasures are always hidden and just those who know the secrets to those treasures have access and thus can benefit from them. The Lord says you already know the secrets. Maybe you just don't know that they are secrets to unlocking the mysteries that are hidden in the word.

It is someone having the key to a treasure house without him knowing that it is the key to such a place. All you need to know is how to apply the secrets you already possess. You are not a stranger! You have the secrets of the house; begin to make use of them. Ask the Holy Spirit-the Revealer of God's mysteries to illuminate the secrets of the Kingdom in your possession, and how to effectively apply them for maximum impact.

Proclaim what you are

Father, I thank you for what You say concerning me. I believe Your word with all my heart and with all my soul. I refuse to believe what my circumstances say. I refuse to believe what people say.

I stand on your word and therefore confess that I am what You say I am. And I am who You say I am.

I have the secrets of the Kingdom in the inside of me. By faith I will draw them out and make use of them to unlock treasures hidden in Your word. I have access to divine mysteries. I will understand the things of the kingdom. What is closed to others is accessible to me. Thank you for such a wondrous gift, in Jesus' Name, amen.

# #
4

EVERYTHING IS YOURS FOR THE ASKING

(Matthew 7:7)

"Ask and it will be given to you; seek and you will find; knock and the door will be opened to you."

Everything you need to have to live life in its fullness in accordance with the will of God is just a request away from you. You just need to ask in faith and it will be yours for the asking. James said, *"You do not have because you do not ask God"* (James 4:2c). I don't care the thing you want, if it agrees with God's word and His plan for you as an individual you can have it if you ask it. I did not say it. He said it in His unfailing word. Didn't He say elsewhere in His holy word that those who seek the Lord lack no good thing? It is written, *"The lions may grow weak and hungry, but those who seek the Lord **lack no good thing**"* (Psalm 34:10). The reason we lack good things is because we seek for the good things. God wants you to seek Him and in seeking Him you will find every good thing. As you seek him your will become aligned to His, and as you ask in accordance with His will it becomes yours, as saint John said, this is the confidence **we** have in approaching God: hat **if we ask anything** according to his will, he hears us (1John 5:14). The emphasis is on anything according to His will.

Proclaim what you are

Father, I thank you for what You say concerning me. I believe Your word with all my heart and with all my soul. I refuse to believe what my circumstances say. I refuse to believe what people say. I stand on your word and therefore confess that I am what You say I am. And I am who You say I am.

I am your son, all I have is yours and all you have is mine for the asking. I reject the beggar's mentality. I will remain in a position where you can always hear me when I ask for anything. I know you are more than willing and ready to give to me. So, I come in faith to make my request known to You, In Jesus Name, amen.

#5

YOU HAVE AUTHORITY TO BIND AND TO LOOSE

(Matthew 18:18)

"I tell you the truth, whatever you bind on earth will be bound in heaven, and whatever you loose on earth will be loosed in heaven."

When the Lord made this startling revelation, He was telling us that we can shape our lives according to the things we want. Whatever is happening to you, which is contrary to the word of God you have the mandate to bind it and render it ineffective. The things which you expect but seem not to come your way you can loose them from whatever may be holding them. You see that what you permit happens and what you refuse ceases to happen. The things which flow freely in heaven but ae hindered on earth have to be loosed to flow here on earth, the things which are not in heaven but which manifest here in earth and hinder the fullness of life you are supposed to live on earth are to be bound. Such is the authority given you to determine the affairs of this planet so that it is in sync with heaven.

Proclaim what you are

Father, I thank you for what You say concerning me. I believe Your word with all my heart and with all my soul. I refuse to believe what my circumstances say. I refuse to believe what people say. I stand on your word and therefore confess that I am what You say I am. And I am who You say I am.

I cannot be bound by what I have not allowed, and I have mandate to loose what I want. In the Name of Jesus, I bind all contrary forces operating in my affairs and environment. I loose my blessings in the spirit realm. I loose angels to go on assignments on my behalf and make things happen in my favour, amen.

# #
6

YOU HAVE THE GENES OF GOD IN YOU

(John 1:12-13)

"Yet to all who received him, to those who believed in his name, he gave the right to become children of God[13] children born not of natural descent, nor of human decision or a husband's will, but born of God."

The child automatically gets the genes of the father. Because you are born of God, you have the genes of God in the inside of you. The genes of wisdom, power, success, and creative ability are all inside of you. From today you should cease to act as a normal person because you are born from above. You can speak things into existence because your Father's genes are in you. Remember He spoke everything into being, and He has transmitted to you those same genes. The next time somebody ask you what you think you are made of; tell him you are made of divine genes.

It is written that, *"For we are members of his body, of his flesh, and of his bones"* (Ephesians 5:30). One thing which is common among the parts of a human body is that all the parts are made of the same genetic material. The genes in the head are the same genes in the feet, the genes in the brain are the same genes in the bowels.

Because you are born of God you are an overcomer. You are able to love without reservation. You are able to forgive all those who sin against you and hurt you. You are able to walk in holiness and righteousness. Because you are born of God you are more than a conqueror, the genes of dominion and rulership are in the inside of you.

Proclaim what you are

Father, I thank you for what You say concerning me. I believe Your word with all my heart and with all my soul. I refuse to believe what my circumstances say. I refuse to believe what people say. I stand on your word and therefore confess that I am what You say I am. And I am who You say I am.

I have your genes in me. I have stored in the inside of me divine wisdom, power, creative ability. Because I am Your child, I will reflect the life from above. I refuse to reason, think, talk, and act like one born of a natural descent. I will speak things that are not as though they were because your creative power resides in me, in Jesus Name, amen.

# #
7

YOU ARE SECURE IN CHRIST

(John 10:28-29)

"I give them eternal life, and they shall never perish; no one can snatch them out of my hand. 29 My Father, who has given them to me, is greater than all, no one can snatch them out of my Father's hand."

Insecurity is one of the maladies which have plagued the world. But for you who are in Christ you are secure from all the threats of the evil one. You are protected both by the hand of the Father and of the Lord Jesus. Your enemies may rage to death but you can be unmoved by their threats because the strongest being in the universe is keeping you. So, stop panicking and relax in the sure protection the Father offers you daily. Serve God with a sense of security that the greater One has your back. He surrounds you with flames of fire. He has build a hedge of protection around you and all that is yours. Remember, *"Ye are of God, little children, and have overcome them: because greater is he that is in you, than he that is in the world"* (1John 4:4). Get up daily and personalize this verse out loud, *"Now unto him that is able to keep you from falling, and to present you faultless before the presence of his glory with exceeding joy, 25 To the only wise God our Saviour, be glory and majesty, dominion and power, both now and ever. Amen"* (Jude 1:24-25).

Proclaim what you are

Father, I thank you for what You say concerning me. I believe Your word with all my heart and with all my soul. I refuse to believe what my circumstances say. I refuse to believe what people say. I stand on your word and therefore confess that I am what You say I am. And I am who You say I am.

I confess that I am secure in You. Nothing can harm me because I am in You and Your hands hold me in You. I refuse to give way to fear even in the midst of storms. I know nothing can snatch me from Your hand. I reject all manner of insecurity in the way I think, speak, and act. I relax in the assurance of Your protection, in Jesus' great Name, amen.

# #
8

YOU HAVE A PREPARED AND GUARANTEED PLACE IN HEAVEN

(John 14:1-2)

"Do not let your hearts be troubled. Trust in God, trust also in me. In my Father's house are many rooms; if it were not so, I would have told you. I am going there to prepare a place for you."

If you are truly born again, you have a place that has been guaranteed you in heaven. Many people do not live effective lives because the devil keeps on bringing in doubt in their minds about their eternal security. The Lord says He has prepared a place for you; very soon He will come to take you to be with Him. So next time the devil comes to question you, tell him to keep off, that you have a guaranteed mansion awaiting you in the Kingdom from which he was shamefully driven. Live daily in accordance with the revealed will of God in His word, and you will have nothing to worry about. For the One who called you is able to keep you to the day of His return.

Proclaim what you are

Father, I thank you for what You say concerning me. I believe Your word with all my heart and with all my soul. I refuse to believe what my circumstances say. I refuse to believe what people say. I stand on your word and therefore confess that I am what You say I am. And I am who You say I am.

I have a place guaranteed in heaven for me. I will live holy and in obedience to you so as to stay in the path that leads me there. I am not a candidate for hell. I am a sure candidate for heaven. On this earth I am but on a pilgrim journey. I refuse to lose sight of my destination, in Jesus' Name, amen.

# #
9

YOU ARE SPIRITUALLY CLEAN

(John 15:3)

"You are already clean because of the word I have spoken to you."

Knowledge of the fact that you are clean because of the word of God which has been spoken to you will keep you from playing with the mud of sin. Just like you will avoid dirt when you know that you are clean, so you will avoid all that contaminates because you know that you have been made clean by the word. James talked of keeping *"oneself from being polluted by the world"*. You have been made clean by the word of God which you listen to. Next time someone invites you into the mud of sin, tell that one you are too clean to play in mud.

Now because you live in a contaminated world, things may rub on you unconsciously, that is why you have to encounter the word through systematic reading, study, and meditation because, as you interact with the word, it washes and cleanses you from impurities. It is written that, *"That he might sanctify and cleanse it with the washing of water by the word"* (Ephesians 5:25). The word has a role in your sanctification!

Proclaim what you are

Father, I thank you for what You say concerning me. I believe Your word with all my heart and with all my soul. I refuse to believe what my circumstances say. I refuse to believe what people say.

I stand on your word and therefore confess that I am what You say I am. And I am who You say I am.

I have been washed, I have been sanctified and justified in Christ. I refuse to play with sin. I will keep away from all that contaminates spirit, soul, and body. I reject the accusations of the evil one regarding my past, in Jesus` Name, amen.

#10

YOU ARE A BRANCH OF THE VINE

(John 15:5)

"I am the vine; you are the branches. If a man remains in me and I in him, he will bear much fruit; apart from me you can do nothing."

The Vine is Jesus, and you are a branch of that Vine. This means you have a permanent connection to the Vine. You are connected to the One who holds all things by the word of his authority, the King of the whole universe. It means that your every supply comes from Him, your very life originates from Him. It is for this reason you should do all not to be separated from the vine.

Also, the branch can only bear fruits according to the type of the vine. So, from today you will not bear any fruit which is not of the vine to which you belong. Refuse to allow the devil to do any kind of grafting in your life. You should and must bear only the fruit of the Spirit.

Proclaim what you are

Father, I thank you for what You say concerning me. I believe Your word with all my heart and with all my soul. I refuse to believe what my circumstances say. I refuse to believe what people say. I stand on your word and therefore confess that I am what You say I am. And I am who You say I am.

I am a branch of the True Vine, I can only bear fruit in keeping with the vine. I refuse the enemy from grafting his branch on me. I shall stay connected to the vine and bring forth the fruit of the Spirit, in Jesus' Name, amen.

# #
11

YOU WERE SPECIALLY CHOSEN BY THE LORD

(John 15:16)

"Ye have not chosen me, but I have chosen you, and ordained you, that ye should go and bring forth fruit, and that your fruit should remain: that whatsoever ye shall ask of the Father in my name, he may give it you"

The choice to belong to the Lord did not originate from you. It was His decision and choice to call you to Himself and make you His son or daughter. Is that not wonderful? Can you imagine that He went through many others in your community and personally hand-picked you out of the many people in you class, workplace, neighbourhood, tribe etc. to make you His own. So, from today henceforth your struggles to keep yourself in Him should stop. Do not try to impress the Lord with your works. He chose you out of His good will and pleasure.

"But after that the kindness and love of God our Saviour toward man appeared, Not by works of righteousness which we have done, but according to his mercy he saved us, by the washing of regeneration, and renewing of the Holy Ghost; Which he shed on us abundantly through Jesus Christ our Saviour" (Titus 3:4-6). He has not changed His choice. You are still the one. The next time you meet someone tell him or her you are a special choice of the Lord's!

The choice was originally based on His grace and mercy only. And I read somewhere that *"It is of the Lord's mercies that we are not consumed, because his compassions fail not. They are new every morning: great is thy faithfulness"* (Lamentations 3:22-23). No matter what you have done, His mercies are new every morning. Do not feel as though God has changed his choice of you. You are still the one he has chosen. Just repent and change your path back to his loving arms. You are his choice!

Proclaim what you are

Father, I thank you for what You say concerning me. I believe Your word with all my heart and. with all my soul. I refuse to believe what my circumstances say. I refuse to believe what people say I stand on your word and therefore confess that I am what You say I am. And I am who You say I am.

I confess that I am special in your sight. I decide to relax in You. I refuse to struggle to keep myself in you. The choice was yours and you have not changed your mind concerning me. Thank you for going through the crowd and singling me out to demonstrate your goodness. amen

# #
12

YOU DO NOT BELONG TO THE WORLD

(John 15:19)

"If you belonged to the world, it would love you as its own. As it is, you do not belong to the world, but I have chosen you out of the world. That is why the world hates you."

Many people think that believers are acting strange. That is true, absolutely true! The simple reason being that they are strangers in this world! A stranger should act strangely, that is why he is called a stranger. From today henceforth you must see yourself as not being a part of this world. If not, you will not keep to your supposed strange actions and behaviour.

Your culture is different from theirs, the reason for which they cannot understand you. The Lord Jesus Christ in His heart rending prayer for the disciples said to the Father, *"They are not of the world, even as I am not of it"* (John 17:16) so from today henceforth you won't compromise anymore! Stop seeking to be accepted by the world. Many people in their quest for worldly acceptance have embraced the standards, ways, and principles of the world. Don't you remember that the system of the world is at enmity with God?

Is it not written that *"Love not the world, neither the things that are in the world. If any man loves the world, the love of the Father is not in him. For all that is in the world, the lust of the flesh, and the lust of the eyes, and the pride of life, is not of the Father, but is of the world. And the* world passeth away, and the lust thereof: but he that doeth the will of God abideth for ever" (1John 2:15-17)?

Proclaim what you are

Father, I thank you for what You say concerning me. I believe Your word with all my heart and. with all my soul. I refuse to believe what my circumstances say. I refuse to believe what people say I stand on your word and therefore confess that I am what You say I am. And I am who You say I am.

I refuse to think, reason, speak and act like the world does. I am set apart from the world and set apart unto God. I will not allow the world to squeeze me into its mold. I will live by the principles of the Kingdom. I will think, reason, speak and act in accordance with the Kingdom I belong to. In Jesus' Name, amen.

# #
13

YOU ARE ENTITLED TO THE HOLY GHOST BAPTISM

(Acts 2:39)

"The promise is for you and your children and for all who are far off--for all whom the Lord our God will call."

As one who has confessed Christ as your Lord and Saviour, you have a right to be baptized by the Holy Spirit. It is the promise of the Father. It is very essential for you to get baptized in the Holy Ghost if you are not yet. You miss a lot by living of life which is not constantly filled by the Spirit. He will teach you to pray and will pray for you in a special language. He will guide you and tell you things you will otherwise not know. Claim this promise; it is your right as one born from above.

Proclaim what you are

Father, I thank you for what You say concerning me. I believe Your word with all my heart and. with all my soul. I refuse to believe what my circumstances say. I refuse to believe what people say I stand on your word and therefore confess that I am what You say I am. And I am who You say I am.

I believe I can't live to my full potential, let alone tap into your potential without the Holy Spirit. I want to be filled with the Holy Spirit, I submit myself to the baptism of the Holy Spirit with evidence of speaking in tongues.

# #
14

YOUR PERIOD AND PLACE OF LIVING WAS PRE-DETERMINED BY GOD

(Acts 17:26)

"From one man he made every nation of men, that they should inhabit the whole earth; and he determined the times set for them and the exact places where they should live."

Before you were born God determined the period for which you should live and the place in which you should live for the greatest impact for His Kingdom. The place where a man stays matters a lot to the accomplishment of his God-ordained destiny. It is your place to ask God where He decided for you to live. There is power in being in the right place geographically. I talked about this in detail in my book *"Fulfilling your Destiny"*.

Proclaim what you are

Father, I thank you for what You say concerning me. I believe Your word with all my heart and with all my soul. I refuse to believe what my circumstances say. I refuse to believe what people say I stand on your word and therefore confess that I am what You say I am. And I am who You say I am.

Lord, I do not want to live my life trying things out. I know you have predetermined where I should live at any one moment in my life. I refuse to move by opportunities and circumstances.

○I will follow your leading as to where to locate or relocate so as to remain in your will and blessing, in Jesus Name, amen.

# #
15

YOU LIVE AND MOVE AND HAVE YOUR BEING IN GOD

(Acts 17:28)

"'For in him we live and move and have our being.' As some of your own poets have said, 'We are his offspring.'"

As a child of God, you live by God, you move by God, you have your being in God. As long as you are alive, you have God in you. He is the very essence of your life. The next time you feel God is very far away, tell yourself that He is near, because as long as you have life, that life originates from Him. Without Him things will fly apart in your life. As you make your choices daily, do it with the consciousness of God working in you and through you, then things will be a lot more different in the positive sense of it.

The prophet Jeremiah confessed, *"O Lord, I know that the path of [life of] a man is not in himself; It is not within [the limited ability of] man [even one at his best] to choose and direct his steps [in life]"* (Jeremiah 10:23, Amp) and the teacher said, *"A man's mind plans his way [as he journeys through life], But the Lord directs his steps and establishes them"* (Proverbs 16:9, Amp) and *"Man's steps are ordered and ordained by the Lord. How then can a man [fully] understand his way?"* (Proverbs 20:24, Amp). God is always in control even of the conscious and unconscious choices you make when in the dark.

Proclaim what you are

Father, I thank you for what You say concerning me. I believe Your word with all my heart and. with all my soul. I refuse to believe what my circumstances say. I refuse to believe what people say I stand on your word and therefore confess that I am what You say I am. And I am who You say I am.

I will follow your leading in all I do, my steps, turns, and stops will be done in pace with your spirit. I refuse to move by my instincts, in Jesus Name. I take every step in this life knowing that you determine the outcome and direct my way. amen.

# #
16

YOU HAVE BEEN FREED FROM SIN

(Romans 6:6-7)

"For we know that our old self was crucified with him so that the body of sin might be done away with, that we should no longer be slaves to sin-- ⁷ because anyone who has died has been freed from sin."

A prisoner who has been granted clemency but is unaware will remain in his prison cell. He might even be tormented by the warders. Sin is a hard task master who will not let go its captives. But freedom was decreed for you the moment you professed Christ from your heart. So, from today henceforth you will no longer allow sin to be your master. You have been made free by the King of the universe and so do not allow anything to keep you captive for any reason. That will be a violation of a royal decree.

Proclaim what you are

Father, I thank you for what You say concerning me. I believe Your word with all my heart and. with all my soul. I refuse to believe what my circumstances say. I refuse to believe what people say. I stand on your word and therefore confess that I am what You say I am. And I am who You say I am.

I declare that I am free from sin. I am dead to sin and therefore I cannot practice sin any longer. I reject the claims of sin over me,

I refuse to yield to its power and appeals. I take my stand in freedom and holiness which Christ has brought to me. In Jesus' name, amen.

# #
17

YOU ARE FREE FROM CONDEMNATION

(Romans 8:1-2)

"Therefore, there is now no condemnation for those who are in Christ Jesus, because through Christ Jesus the law of the Spirit of life set me free from the law of sin and death."

Because you are in Christ Jesus, who is your advocate, you are no longer under condemnation. In fact, you have been immune from all manner of condemnation because of your allegiance to the King. All charges that were held against you wear dropped the moment you took the decision to follow Christ. Do not let the devil accuse you any longer. The next time he comes with his railing accusations tell him he is living behind time because Christ Jesus bore the condemnation on your behalf.

Proclaim what you are

Father, I thank you for what You say concerning me. I believe Your word with all my heart and. with all my soul. I refuse to believe what my circumstances say. I refuse to believe what people say I stand on your word and therefore confess that I am what You say I am. And I am who You say I am.

There is now no condemnation over my life. I have been forgiven, cleansed, justified and restored. I rebuke every voice of accusation. I have been declared not guilty, set free and shielded by the law of the Spirit of life. I refuse to operate under the law of condemnation, in Jesus Name, amen.

# #
18

YOU ARE CONTROLLED BY THE SPIRIT

(Romans 8:9)

"You, however, are controlled not by the sinful nature but by the Spirit, if the Spirit of God lives in you. And if anyone does not have the Spirit of Christ, he does not belong to Christ."

Paul says here that if the Spirit of God lives in you then it is He who controls you. The leading of the Spirit can become interwoven into your normal life that you may not even be aware that He is leading you. But, actually, it is He who leads you to take every correct decision and right step you have ever taken. Paul says that you are controlled by the Spirit and not that you can be or will be, but that you currently are being controlled by Him because He lives in you. Isn't that wonderful? That you can live in the consciousness that your life is controlled by the Holy Spirit so that you can actively yield to his leading, promptings, and nudging?

Proclaim what you are

Father, I thank you for what You say concerning me. I believe Your word with all my heart and. with all my soul. I refuse to believe what my circumstances say. I refuse to believe what people say I stand on your word and therefore confess that I am what You say I am. And I am who You say I am.

I am a spirit being, with a soul, living in a body. I am not led by the flesh but by the Spirit. I yield continuously to the Spirit, I will listen and follow no other voice but that of the Spirit. I will make my choices and take decisions in accordance to what the Spirit is saying, in Jesus Name, amen.

# #
19

YOUR PRESENT SUFFERING CANNOT COMPARE TO THE GLORY AWAITING YOU

(Romans 8:18)

"I consider that our present sufferings are not worth comparing with the glory that will be revealed in us."

As a Christian there is much you have decided to give up in the form of pleasure or other things. There are some pains you bear which will otherwise not have come to you had you not been a Christian. However, all what you have gone through or are going through and will go through put together cannot compare with the glory that is awaiting you because of the suffering you are enduring for His Name sake.

Proclaim what you are

Father, I thank you for what You say concerning me. I believe Your word with all my heart and. with all my soul. I refuse to believe what my circumstances say. I refuse to believe what people say I stand on your word and therefore confess that I am what You say I am. And I am who You say I am.

Every suffering that comes my way because of the cross, because of the cost of following you, I will accept and embrace. Whatever I may endure, for the cause of the gospel, cannot compare with the glory that comes because of it. I will not seek suffering, but I won't run away from it either because I know You are always with me and will lead me through each step victoriously. In Jesus Name, amen.

# #
20

ALL OF CREATION IS AWAITING YOUR MANIFESTATION

(Romans 8:19)

"The creation waits in eager expectation for the sons of God to be revealed."

The children of God have much role to play during these end times. All of creation is eagerly waiting for your manifestation as a child of God. You have been in hiding for too long.

It is time to come out of your hiding place and do exploits for your God and His Christ. It is time for you to manifest that which God has deposited in you. Creation is in bondage to the devil and seeks her release. We as the children of God are the ones to bring liberty to the rest of creation still in bondage. When they look at you, they long to see you manifest the power and glory God has deposited in you. From today know that many things are waiting for you to begin manifesting. The destiny of creation is tied to your manifestation, to be brought into the glorious liberty of the accomplishments of the cross of Calvary. Say it out loud, *"it is the season of my manifestation, my light is shining brighter and brighter. I am revealing heaven on earth"*.

Proclaim what you are

Father, I thank you for what You say concerning me. I believe Your word with all my heart and. with all my soul. I refuse to believe what my circumstances say. I refuse to believe what people say I stand on your word and therefore confess that I am what You say I am. And I am who You say I am.

I will fulfil my destiny and not forfeit it. I will be manifested to my generation. My generation shall be pleased with my manifestation because it waits in eager expectation for me. Eyes shall behold the wonder of your working in me and rejoice at what you have made of me. I shall be an amazement to the ordinary mind in Jesus' Name, amen.

# #
21

THE SPIRIT INTERCEDES FOR YOU

(Romans 8:26-27)

"In the same way, the Spirit helps us in our weakness. We do not know what we ought to pray for, but the Spirit himself intercedes for us with groans that words cannot express. And he who searches our hearts knows the mind of the Spirit, because the Spirit intercedes for the saints in accordance with God's will."

You have a constant all knowing intercessor who prays for you in accordance with the will of God for your life. This means that His prayers for you cannot go unanswered since He knows the mind of the Father concerning you. It is for this reason you must practice praying in the Spirit always because as you give Him the opportunity He will pray through you, for you and for others. I personally pray in the Spirit for at least two hours during my normal prayer sessions. When you do not know what to pray just let Him pray through you in unknown words. Pray intentionally for situations with unknown words. When you yield yourself to Him, He will pray with an intensity that words cannot express.

Proclaim what you are

Father, I thank you for what You say concerning me. I believe Your word with all my heart and. with all my soul. I refuse to believe what my circumstances say. I refuse to believe what people say

I stand on your word and therefore confess that I am what You say I am. And I am who You say I am.

Lord, I thank you for the unfailing intercession of the Holy Spirit on my behalf. Thank you that every prayer of His on my behalf is answered. I will give Him more opportunities to intercede for me by praying in the spirit often and always. In Jesus Name, amen.

# #
22

ALL THINGS WORK TOGETHER FOR YOUR GOOD

(Romans 8:28)

"And we know that in all things God works for the good of those who love him who have been called according to his purpose."

This is wonderful to know, that even the ill intentions of the devil towards you will turn out to work for your good as long as you are a lover of God. The devil does not have the final say in your life. No matter what he does it is the Almighty Jesus who has the final say, that is, it is Him who determines the outcome of whatever may come your way. You can take whatever combination of things which have happened to you. God says all those things will turn out for your good. Cease to glorify the devil by giving him credit for the things that are allowed into your life. Acknowledge the sovereignty and centrality of Christ Jesus in your life. Each time you give the devil credit you are condemning yourself as one who does not love God. If you indeed love the love, there is one thing you can bet your life on, that in all things God will work it out for your good.

Proclaim what you are

Father, I thank you for what You say concerning me. I believe Your word with all my heart and. with all my soul. I refuse to believe what my circumstances say. I refuse to believe what people say

I stand on your word and therefore confess that I am what You say I am. And I am who You say I am.

Lord, I believe that nothing happens to me by chance because my life is in Your hands. I believe that You work in everything that happens in my life for the ultimate good of Your eternal purpose for my life. I love You Lord, I am called according to Your purpose, therefore in all things You are working for my good, in Jesus Name, amen.

# #
23

BECAUSE GOD IS FOR YOU, IT DOESN'T MATTER WHO IS AGAINST YOU

(Romans 8:31)

"What, then, shall we say in response to this? If God is for us, who can be against us?"

You have the strongest Person, the highest Authority, the best Judge, the greatest Advocate, the wisest Person, the most loving Person on your side. Now does it matter who is on the other side? Certainly, it doesn't. Let the devil go to hell before his time if he so desires, you care not for Him because God and you are the majority and you make the strongest team there can ever be.

Let the devil hit the ceiling if he wills, his opposition counts for nothing. You will live to meet much opposition in life but the heart knowledge that God is in you, with you and for you will make you a perpetual victor. If God is for your marriage, it doesn't matter who is against it. If God is for your success and uplifting let all hell be let loose, it counts for nothing.

Proclaim what you are

Father, I thank you for what You say concerning me. I believe Your word with all my heart and. with all my soul. I refuse to believe what my circumstances say. I refuse to believe what people say I stand on your word and therefore confess that I am what You say I am. And I am who You say I am.

Lord, forgive me for when I have thought I was alone. Forgive me for the times when I was afraid and cowered before opposition. From henceforth I face challenges knowing that because You are with me no challenge can defeat me. With you I am unstoppable. With you I indomitable. In Jesus' name, amen.

# #
24

NOTHING CAN SEPARATE YOU FROM GOD'S LOVE

(Romans 8:35-39)

"35 Who shall separate us from the love of Christ? Shall trouble or hardship or persecution or famine or nakedness or danger or sword? 36 As it is written:
"For your sake we face death all day long;
we are considered as sheep to be slaughtered."
37 No, in all these things we are more than conquerors through him who loved us. 38 For I am convinced that neither death nor life, neither angels nor demons, neither the present nor the future, nor any powers, 39 neither height nor depth, nor anything else in all creation, will be able to separate us from the love of God that is in Christ Jesus our Lord."

Romans 8:37

Is it not wonderful to know that God's love for you is everlasting? Is it not comforting and breathe-taking to realise that nothing in this world can separate you from God' love; whether things in the visible or the invisible, just nothing? You can rest assured of the fact that nothing external can sever that love relationship. The relationship was initiated, and is sustained, by Him. You can relax and enjoy that never-ending love.

Proclaim what you are

Father, I thank you for what You say concerning me. I believe Your word with all my heart and. with all my soul. I refuse to believe what my circumstances say. I refuse to believe what people say I stand on your word and therefore confess that I am what You say I am. And I am who You say I am.

Lord, I believe nothing can separate me from You, nothing can separate me from your love. I am surrounded by and engulfed in your love. I will be conscious of this fact every day and in everything. In Jesus Name, amen.

# #
25

CHRIST HAS BECOME YOUR RIGHTEOUSNESS AND HOLINESS

(1Corinthians 1:30)

"It is because of him that you are in Christ Jesus, who has become for us wisdom from God--that is, our righteousness, holiness and redemption."

Because you have professed Christ and are living in Him, He is your righteousness and holiness before the Father. When the Father looks at you He sees the righteousness and holiness of His Son in you and on you and therefore reckons you righteous in His sight. Therefore, if anyone should ask you why you are confident that you are not a sinner, tell him that Christ Jesus has become your righteousness and holiness before God. You are a righteous and holy person, but that is not of yourself but of God. This should make you confident and make you understand your victory over sin.

Proclaim what you are

Father, I thank you for what You say concerning me. I believe Your word with all my heart and. with all my soul. I refuse to believe what my circumstances say. I refuse to believe what people say I stand on your word and therefore confess that I am what You say I am. And I am who You say I am.

I believe I am righteous and holy because Christ Jesus has become my righteousness and holiness in you. I refuse the circumstances surrounding me, I choose to believe what you say, in Jesus Name, amen.

# #
26

YOU HAVE BEEN WASHED, SANCTIFIED AND JUSTIFIED

(1Corinthians 6:11)

"And that is what some of you were. But you were washed, you were sanctified, you were justified in the name of the Lord Jesus Christ and by the Spirit of our God."

Many people still live with the guilt of their past sins and this makes them afraid to claim their rights as children of God. Listen, whatever you were before you came to Christ, if you have repented and carried out restitution where it was needed, do not let the devil trouble you any longer with accusations. You have been washed by the blood and appear sinless before the Father. Because you have been washed you cannot afford to play with the mud of sin any longer. Stay clean in your sanctification.

Proclaim what you are

Father, I thank you for what You say concerning me. I believe Your word with all my heart and. with all my soul. I refuse to believe what my circumstances say. I refuse to believe what people say. I stand on your word and therefore confess that I am what You say I am. And I am who You say I am.

I will keep myself pure and free from pollution. I refuse to play with any form of sin, in Jesus' Name, amen.

# #
27

YOUR BODY IS GOD'S TEMPLE

(1Corinthians 6:19)

"Do you not know that your body is a temple of the Holy Spirit, who is in you, whom you have received from God? You are not your own."

You are a living habitation of the Godhead; Father, Son, and Holy Spirit are all living in you, therefore your body is sacred. You cannot afford to desecrate that which the Father has made sacred by His own very presence. My prayer is that your view concerning that body should change from *"my body"* to *"God's temple"*. When this happens, you will ensure that you keep out of that sacred place anything which can bring defilement. You will treat that temple with holy reverence because of the One who lives in it.

Proclaim what you are

Father, I thank you for what You say concerning me. I believe Your word with all my heart and. with all my soul. I refuse to believe what my circumstances say. I refuse to believe what people say I stand on your word and therefore confess that I am what You say I am. And I am who You say I am.

I will keep my temple sacred, by the power of the Holy Spirit. Every unclean thing will stay out of this temple. I will keep a watch over its gates and make sure nothing that defiles enters it, in Jesus' Name, amen.

# #
28

YOU HAVE BEEN ANOINTED AND SEALED BY GOD

(2 Corinthians 1:21-22, Ephesians 1:13)

"Now it is God who makes both us and you stand firm in Christ. He anointed us, set his seal of ownership on us, and put his Spirit in our hearts as a deposit, guaranteeing what is to come."
"And you also were included in Christ when you heard the word of truth, the gospel of your salvation. Having believed, you were marked in him with a seal, the promised Holy Spirit"

The moment you believed, God anointed you and put His seal of ownership on you. This makes any claim of the devil over your life to be false. The seal of God upon your life tells the devil that you are a no-go-zone for him and his cohorts. In fact, it is the seal of the Father that makes the angels recognise you. It sets you apart even when you are in a crowd of sinners in the busiest place of the planet. Your having the seal of God on you should make you bold and confident in whatever circumstance you find your self. Satanists recognise that seal and keep off. They may want to make you afraid if you do not know that God's seal is on you. But because you now know about the seal, you can mock at their rage!

Also, you have been anointed to provide solution to the dilemmas of life wherever you are. Get up every day and declare, *"The Spirit of the Lord is upon me, because he hath anointed me to preach the gospel to the poor; he hath sent me to heal the broken-hearted, to preach deliverance to the captives, and recovering of sight to the blind, to set at liberty them that are bruised"* (Luke 4:18). You have been anointed for exploits. You have been anointed for healing, deliverance, and breakthrough. See yourself as a divine solution to common problems plaguing mankind.

Proclaim what you are

Father, I thank you for what You say concerning me. I believe Your word with all my heart and. with all my soul. I refuse to believe what my circumstances say. I refuse to believe what people say I stand on your word and therefore confess that I am what You say I am. And I am who You say I am.

Thank you for anointing me, and for sealing me as your own. I reject all claims of the devil over me or my affairs. By the anointing on me I break every yoke of the evil one over my life or property, in Jesus' Name, amen.

# #
29

CHRIST DIED FOR YOU SO THAT YOU MAY LIVE FOR HIM

(2Corinthians 5:15)

"And he died for all, that those who live should no longer live for themselves but for him who died for them and was raised again."

True satisfaction and fulfilment can only come to you, your life can only have meaning, when you stop living for yourself and start living for another. That another is the One who died to free you from the dominion of sin and the devil. Your life only finds purpose and direction when you devote it for the service of the King. All else can only bring phoney short-term satisfaction. From today decide that you will live all of your life for God, by Christ Jesus. That is the only way for you to find satisfaction. Remember, *"And whatsoever ye do, do it heartily, as to the Lord, and not unto men"* (Colossians 3:23).

Proclaim what you are

Father, I thank you for what You say concerning me. I believe Your word with all my heart and. with all my soul. I refuse to believe what my circumstances say. I refuse to believe what people say I stand on your word and therefore confess that I am what You say I am. And I am who You say I am.

Lord, I refuse to live for myself henceforth. I denounce and renounce all my self-centred pursuits and decide to live for you, in the choices I make and in the things, I expend myself for, in Jesus Name, amen.

# #
30

YOU ARE A NEW CREATURE IN CHRIST

(2 Corinthians 5:17)

"Therefore, if anyone is in Christ, he is a new creation; the old has gone, the new has come!"

You have been made new by the new birth. Old things are past away and God has given you a new heart, a new spirit, a new purpose, a new family. You now have a new Master, a new Father, and a new home. You are in deed a new creation in Christ Jesus. Concerning you God has made all things new, even your record in heaven is a new record. Your future is a new one, for before the new birth you had another future which was bleak and uncertain. But because of the new birth you have a bright new future in Christ. Do not allow any man to judge you according to your past. Each time the devil accuses you of your past, tell him he's mistaken, the old man is dead, you are a brand-new creature of God's. You have been remade and remodelled according to the divine.

Proclaim what you are

Father, I thank you for what You say concerning me. I believe Your word with all my heart and. with all my soul. I refuse to believe what my circumstances say. I refuse to believe what people say I stand on your word and therefore confess that I am what You say I am. And I am who You say I am.

I am a new creature in Christ, separated from my past, living a new life in Christ, destined for a bright future, in Jesus Name, amen.

# #
31

YOU ARE CHRIST'S AMBASSADOR

(2Corinthians 5:20)

"We are therefore Christ's ambassadors, as though God were making his appeal through us. We implore you on Christ's behalf: Be reconciled to God."

Wherever you are on this planet, you are an ambassador for the Kingdom. You are a legal and authorised representative of the King on this dark planet. You are permitted to issue as many permanent resident visas as you see the need. Because you are an ambassador, it is your home country's responsibility to take charge of all your needs. So, from today, know that all of heaven's resources are at your disposal. As an ambassador you have special guards watching over you. This places a responsibility to know the stance of your home land on every issue, so that you can only do things and give accord in accordance with the principles of your homeland. All of the homelands principles are reveal in the Book. And you have the secret codes to decode what is there and interpret it accordingly. You are not just any kind of person. So, from today begin to live as a diplomat, talk like a diplomat and behave like one.

Proclaim what you are

Father, I thank you for what You say concerning me. I believe Your word with all my heart and. with all my soul. I refuse to

believe what my circumstances say. I refuse to believe what people say I stand on your word and therefore confess that I am what You say I am. And I am who You say I am.

Thank you, Lord, for all you have put at my disposal as an ambassador of the Kingdom. Thank you for immunity from above, thank you for angels commissioned to guard and protect me. I will fulfil my duties as an ambassador. I will seek the interests of the Kingdom and not my personal interests, in the Name of Jesus, amen.

# #
32

YOU ARE BLESSED

(Galatians 3:9,14)

"So those who have faith are blessed along with Abraham, the man of faith…He redeemed us in order that the blessing given to Abraham might come to the Gentiles through Christ Jesus, so that by faith we might receive the promise of the Spirit."

The purpose for which Christ redeemed you is that you should inherit the blessing. That, what was given to Abraham may come to you in its fullness. Because you have faith, you have been blessed along with Abraham. Stop living out of the blessing God has given you. Appropriate and enter into all that the Father has decreed about you. What deprives you of the blessed live is ignorance of the fact that you are already abundantly blessed. You are blessed and highly favoured.

It is written that, *"blessed be the God and Father of our Lord Jesus Christ, who hath blessed us with all spiritual blessings in heavenly places in Christ"* (Ephesians 1:3). I would like you to say it to yourself until you are convinced that you are already abundantly blessed. As soon as you become convinced in the spirit, the blessing will begin flowing to you. It is unbelief that blocks its flow. Faith and consciousness are what translate the blessings from the spiritual into the natural. Because you are blessed, you cannot be cursed. You are not only blessed, you have been made a blessing. Set out everyday with the consciousness that you are a blessing to everyone and everything you encounter.

Proclaim what you are

Father, I thank you for what You say concerning me. I believe Your word with all my heart and. with all my soul. I refuse to believe what my circumstances say. I refuse to believe what people say I stand on your word and therefore confess that I am what You say I am. And I am who You say I am.

Lord I am a candidate for the blessings that you gave to Abraham, by faith I walk into each one of them. I refuse to live in lack. I receive the fullness of your blessing in every domain of my life. I am blessed and I am a blessing, in the Name of Jesus, amen.

# #
33

YOU ARE ABRAHAM'S SEED

(Galatians 3:29)

"If you belong to Christ, then you are Abraham's seed, and heirs according to the promise."

Because you belong to Christ Jesus, you are reckoned to be Abraham's seed. And because you are reckoned to be Abraham's seed, you are an heir to all that was offered Abraham by God. You are an heir to his faith so, begin to exercise faith and live by faith. You are an heir to his obedience so, begin to exercise obedience in all that the Father requires of you. You are an heir to that special relationship he enjoyed with God, so you too can be close to God in a special way. You are an heir to his blessing and so live the blessed life.

Proclaim what you are

Father, I thank you for what You say concerning me. I believe Your word with all my heart and. with all my soul. I refuse to believe what my circumstances say. I refuse to believe what people say I stand on your word and therefore confess that I am what You say I am. And I am who You say I am.

I am a seed of Abraham and therefore an heir to all the promises made to him. I will inherit my possession; I refuse to settle for anything less, I decide to press into the fullness of my inheritance, in Jesus' Name, amen.

# #
34

YOU HAVE EVERY SPIRITUAL BLESSING YOU NEED

(Ephesians 1:3)

"Praise be to the God and Father of our Lord Jesus Christ, who has blessed us in the heavenly realms with every spiritual blessing in Christ."

God has blessed you spiritually with all the spiritual blessing you need for life. Stop praying for blessing and start enjoying the blessing. Everything you need for your spiritual wellbeing has been made available to you. You can rise to any height you want spiritually because God has so designed it. From today you will cease to live in spiritual poverty and lack, in the Name of Jesus. Being a spiritual dwarf has come to an end for you today. Because of this knowledge you shall rise to heights you never experienced before. Faith is the rail on which things move from the spirit realm to the physical. Expectation is what connects you to that realm. Allow your expectations to grow and your faith to grow and be strong. In this way the things kept for you in the heavenly realm will flow to you.

Proclaim what you are

Father, I thank you for what You say concerning me. I believe Your word with all my heart and. with all my soul. I refuse to believe what my circumstances say. I refuse to believe what people say

I stand on your word and therefore confess that I am what You say I am. And I am who You say I am.

Lord, I will allow expectations to grow within me, expectations for great things, and expectations for supernatural things. Fill me with faith from above, even as I respond to your word that I hear, in Jesus' Name, amen.

# #
35

YOU ARE SEATED WITH CHRIST IN THE HEAVENLY PLACES

(Ephesians 2:6)

"And God raised us up with Christ and seated us with him in the heavenly realms in Christ Jesus."

Do you know where Christ is seated? The Bible says He is seated at the right hand of God the Father, far above all rule, power and dominion, and every title that can be given (Ephesians 1:21). So, if you are seated with Christ, then all what there is with respect to Christ's sitting position is also true with respect to your sitting position. This is most humbling but true anyway. You cannot afford to allow the devil threaten you with his lies any longer. You have been placed far above him and all his cohorts. So next time he wants you to come down from your position and meet him down where he is in the place of compromise, tell him you cannot come down to his level. You are seated with Christ in the place of power and authority. Maintain your place and live the life of the heavenly places.

Proclaim what you are

Father, I thank you for what You say concerning me. I believe Your word with all my heart and. with all my soul. I refuse to believe what my circumstances say. I refuse to believe what people say I stand on your word and therefore confess that I am what You say I am. And I am who You say I am.

From today henceforth Lord, I will live and operate from the position of authority you have placed me in. thank you for placing the enemy and his cohorts under my feet, in Jesus' name, amen.

# #
36

YOU ARE A CITIZEN OF HEAVEN

(Ephesians 2:19; Philippians 3:20)

"Consequently, you are no longer foreigners and aliens, but fellow citizens with God's people and members of God's household"
"But our citizenship is in heaven. And we eagerly await a Savior from there, the Lord Jesus Christ"

Because your Father is the King of heaven, and you are born from above, that makes you a citizen of heaven. And because you are a citizen of heaven you live your life based on the rules and laws of the country of your citizenship. You have a legal right to all that heaven offers her citizens. Because heaven is sovereign, your citizenship is also sovereign. You cannot be deported for any reason because heaven is your homeland.

No matter what you do, you can only be disciplined by your home country. Can the government of United States deport her own citizen? If so to where? Heaven does not exile her citizens. So, live by the rules and enjoy the freedom of your heavenly citizenship. As a citizen of heaven, you can go beyond national borders and influence situations because the Kingdom runs across every nation or planet, known and unknown.

Proclaim what you are

Father, I thank you for what You say concerning me. I believe Your word with all my heart and. with all my soul. I refuse to believe what my circumstances say. I refuse to believe what people say I stand on your word and therefore confess that I am what You say I am. And I am who You say I am.

Open my eyes Lord to all my rights and privileges as a citizen of heaven and help me explore all the resources heaven has placed at my disposal as a citizen, in Jesus' Name, amen.

# #
37

GOD WHO STARTED HIS WORK IN YOU WILL BRING IT TO COMPLETION

(Philippians 1:6; 1 Thessalonians 2:13)

"Being confident of this, that he who began a good work in you will carry it on to completion until the day of Christ Jesus."
"And we also thank God continually because, when you received the word of God, which you heard from us, you accepted it not as the word of men, but as it actually is, the word of God, which is at work in you who believe."

God is never involved in half-finished projects. You are a divine project, and what God has started in you and through you will be brought to completion in His own time. He is too faithful to leave you uncompleted. Before He started the project, He counted the cost and saw that He has all it takes to complete His work in you. He has not yet, and will never, run out of patience as far as you are concerned. You are an edifice in the making; your architect is not yet through with you. When someone points at your weakness the next time, tell him or her that God is not yet through with you. By the time he will be through with you, others will marvel at what He has made of you. God who started the work of sanctification, deliverance, salvation, healing and blessing will carry it on to completion. You have not yet reached the height God ordained for you. He is still in the process of lifting you and propelling you to the place He ordained for you. Live daily in the consciousness that God who started the good work in you is still on you, doing what only he can do.

Proclaim what you are

Father, I thank you for what You say concerning me. I believe Your word with all my heart and. with all my soul. I refuse to believe what my circumstances say. I refuse to believe what people say I stand on your word and therefore confess that I am what You say I am. And I am who You say I am.

Thank You because you will never abandon a project of yours. Thank you because you are still working on me. I yield myself to your working. Mold me, shape me, prune me, and file me as you see the need Lord, and let me become the vessel fit for your continuous use, in Jesus Name, amen.

# #
38

YOU HAVE BEEN QUALIFIED TO SHARE IN THE INHERITANCE OF THE SAINTS

(Colossians 1:12)

"Giving thanks to the Father, who has qualified you to share in the inheritance of the saints in the kingdom of light."

Many people seek qualified people to get into certain positions. But God has qualified those He has called to inherit what He has kept in store for the saints. It is God who has qualified you and not your works. If you want to be honest with yourself, the many people around you who are not yet saved may be living far better lives morally speaking than you did while an unbeliever. In human terms they could have been more qualified for salvation and blessing than you. But God chose to qualify you. When you feel inadequate, remind yourself that it is God Himself who qualified you for His blessings.

No one can disqualify you on the basis of your weakness. When God was qualifying you, He saw those weaknesses anyway but decide to cast His strength over them such that He Himself does not take note. When the devil or any of his human or spirit agents accuse you of not being qualified, tell them your qualification comes from God. Also, you must seek trying to qualify yourself, yield to God and by His leading he will qualify you for what He has in store for you.

Proclaim what you are

Father, I thank you for what You say concerning me. I believe Your word with all my heart and. with all my soul. I refuse to believe what my circumstances say. I refuse to believe what people say I stand on your word and therefore confess that I am what You say I am. And I am who You say I am.

Father, I yield to Your leading. I cease trying to make myself qualified. My qualification is in you and I know You have qualified me to inherit the blessings you have for the saints, in Jesus' Name, amen.

# #
39

GOD HAS BROUGHT YOU INTO THE KINGDOM OF CHRIST

(Colossians 1:13)

"For he has rescued us from the dominion of darkness and brought us into the kingdom of the Son he loves"

In the physical, when a man seeks safety under the jurisdiction of another ruler, no matter what he has done, his former ruler needs permission from the present ruler before he can be touched in any way, especially if he has sought for asylum. We too have sought for asylum in the Kingdom of Christ. We have come under His jurisdiction. We are now in the domain of the greatest King. Thus, satan our former master has no power over us any longer. We have been granted asylum so he cannot bring his charges in the court of our King.

Whatever those charges are they shall be thrown out of the court because our accuser has no right to stand in the court of our land. He has no right to exercise his dominion over us. All his claims are illegal because we are in the Kingdom of Another and have been granted citizenship. You are free from the dominion of darkness and are now under the dominion of Light. The King James version says we have been brought into the kingdom of His marvellous light. Light penetrates darkness and darkness can never penetrate light. See your self as untouchable by satan. Decree and proclaim your immunity from his rule and influence.

Proclaim what you are

Father, I thank you for what You say concerning me. I believe Your word with all my heart and. with all my soul. I refuse to believe what my circumstances say. I refuse to believe what people say I stand on your word and therefore confess that I am what You say I am. And I am who You say I am.

Thank You for placing me in a new jurisdiction where the enemy has no right and no access. I will live daily conscious of my immunity from the punishment of my former master because Christ Jesus has become my new Master and King, in Jesus Name, amen.

# #
40

YOU ARE HOLY AND DEARLY LOVED
(Colossians 3:12)

"Therefore, as God's chosen people, holy and dearly loved, clothe yourselves with compassion, kindness, humility, gentleness and patience."

Do you believe you are dearly loved?

Now do you believe you are holy? I can see you hesitating to answer. The same verse which says you are dearly loved is the same verse which says you are holy. In fact, the holiness aspect of it comes before dearly loved aspect. So, you must believe both. God says you are holy and dearly loved. The next time you feel unloved, proclaim loud and clear to the hearing of hell that you are dearly loved. The next time someone accuses you of anything you have repented of, shout out that you are holy.

It is time believers confess and declare that which God has already declared about them. God says you are holy and dearly loved, and that is what He has made of you. He will never say something about you, which He has not already done on your behalf. If I were you I will shout it out *"I am holy and dearly loved"*. The writer of Hebrews says it again, *"therefore holy brothers…"* (Hebrews 3:1). You are a holy brother or sister. That is how the word addresses you.

Proclaim what you are

Father, I thank you for what You say concerning me. I believe Your word with all my heart and. with all my soul. I refuse to believe what my circumstances say. I refuse to believe what people say I stand on your word and therefore confess that I am what You say I am. And I am who You say I am.

Lord I thank you for making me holy, I pledge to follow your leading so as to remain holy. I refuse to let sin have dominion over me. I will, by the power of the Holy spirit maintain my state of holiness, in Jesus Name, amen.

# #
41

GOD WILL STRENGTHEN AND PROTECT YOU

(2 Thessalonians 3:3)

"But the Lord is faithful, and he will strengthen and protect you from the evil one."

This means that there is strength available for you each time you feel weak. The Lord has said He will strengthen you and protect you. This means that there are times when you will lack strength and come under danger. So, the next time you feel weak, it is not strange, just tap into the promise for strength and be strengthened. The next time you feel threatened by whatever, relax in the promised protection of God. There is an infinite reserve of strength for you each time you feel deficient and threatened. Is there any area of your life you need divine strength? Then receive the strength in the name of Jesus and operate with the strength from above. Heaven is watching over you for protection. Live daily with the consciousness of divine protection.

Proclaim what you are

Father, I thank you for what You say concerning me. I believe Your word with all my heart and. with all my soul. I refuse to believe what my circumstances say. I refuse to believe what people say I stand on your word and therefore confess that I am what You say I am. And I am who You say I am.

I will not depend on my own strength for anything but will tap into the fullness of your strength and trust daily in your divine protection over all that concerns me, in Jesus' Name, amen.

# #
42

YOU HAVE THE SPIRIT OF POWER, LOVE, AND BOLDNESS

(2 Timothy 1:7, KJV)

"For God hath not given us the spirit of fear; but of power, and of love, and of a sound mind"

You have the Spirit of power in you. You must cease to live like a weakling because you are not a weakling. Fearfulness and cowardice should not be part of you because you have been given the Spirit of boldness. The Bible says the righteous are as bold as a lion (Proverbs 28:1). Do you know your Father is the Lion of the tribe of Judah? So then, if you are His offspring, you too have the genes of the Lion in you. A lion is never afraid, even when it is alone amongst other animals. It is time you develop the lion in the inside of you. Don't leave it dormant and chained any longer. Let loose that lion in you and let it deal with the foxes eating your life. Put away timidity and be in control for you have been endowed with the Spirit of boldness.

Get up daily and proclaim that you have a sound mind. Confusion should not be part of you. Whenever you feel confused quickly rebuke it and declare that you have a sound mind and tap into the mind of Christ. For it is written that we have the mind of Christ.

Proclaim what you are

Father, I thank you for what You say concerning me. I believe Your word with all my heart and. with all my soul. I refuse to

believe what my circumstances say. I refuse to believe what people say I stand on your word and therefore confess that I am what You say I am. And I am who You say I am.

I reject all forms of fear and doubt. I refuse to harbour any manner of confusion because I have a sound mind. I will walk in love because I have the spirit of love in the inside of me, in Jesus' Name, amen.

43

YOU ARE A ROYAL PRIEST

(1 Peter 2:9)

"But you are a chosen people, a royal priesthood, a holy nation, a people belonging to God, that you may declare the praises of him who called you out of darkness into his wonderful light."

You are not just a priest but a royal priest; one who comes from a royal family and serves the King of the universe. You can forgive sins and you can call people to account. You have the right to intercede for others and God will hear you.

Just as the priests were clothed with dignity in the physical, so are you clothed with dignity in the spiritual. You can get into the holy of holies. You have been clothed with royalty to serve royalty. From today may you use nothing of yours to serve the devil. All what you have must be brought into your service of royalty. Angels look at you in the spiritual and marvel at what God has made of you.

Demons look at you and weep of what they have been striped of because of their rebellion. That is why they are so mad and depraved. You see, lately, I have been pondering why God did not destroy satan at once, then I came to realise that the greatest punishment God has given satan is to leave him existent. Each passing day gets him more depraved and tormented in his soul because he is out of that place of glory. Hell was made for him just because of mankind, so that one day he will cease to deceive the sons of men.

Proclaim what you are

Father, I thank you for what You say concerning me. I believe Your word with all my heart and. with all my soul. I refuse to believe what my circumstances say. I refuse to believe what people say I stand on your word and therefore confess that I am what You say I am. And I am who You say I am.

Thank you for making me royalty to serve royalty. I will carry out my priestly duties of intercession and reconciliation. I shall bless your people with my words and actions, and I will serve You with all that I am and have, for You are the source of all things, in Jesus Name, amen.

# #
44

YOU HAVE EVERYTHING YOU NEED FOR LIFE AND GODLINESS

(2Peter 1:3)

"His divine power has given us everything we need for life and godliness through our knowledge of him who called us by his own glory and goodness."

The power of God that is in you has given you everything you need for your natural life and your spiritual life. Unless you know this, you cannot live up to it. There is nothing which God has not made available to you so that your life can be effective and productive. Are they blessings you need, they have been provided you. Is it power, it has been given you. Is it good health, it has been given you. Is it authority, it has been given you.

Everything has been made available for you. And through His precious promises you can get all you need. It is as you appropriate the promises by faith that you come to the realisation that all has indeed been made available for you. The for you to get access into all that has been made available to you is through your knowledge of God and His Christ. Your knowledge of Him is your key to all you need. That is why you must explore all the avenues you can, as revealed in the Word, to know God. The quality of your life is a function of your knowledge of Him who called you by His own glory and goodness.

Proclaim what you are

Father, I thank you for what You say concerning me. I believe Your word with all my heart and. with all my soul. I refuse to believe what my circumstances say. I refuse to believe what people say I stand on your word and therefore confess that I am what You say I am. And I am who You say I am.

I give myself to seek You and to find you and to know you. Help me explore all available avenues to know you better, in Jesus' name, amen.

# #
45

YOU HAVE OVERCOME THE EVIL ONE

(1 John 2:13b)

"I write to you, young men, because you have overcome the evil one."

The evil one was not only overcome for you; the Bible says you have overcome the evil one. How did it happen? When Christ went to the cross, you were inside of Him, when He died, you too died. When He was buried, you were buried with Him and when He rose victoriously, you rose with Him. It is the resurrection that has given you victory over the evil one. Take note that this victory is already accomplished. So, the devil is a defeated foe over whom you have been given authority.

When Jesus knocked him out on the cross, you were in Christ knocking the devil out. This is not a conditional statement, but an accomplished feat.

Proclaim what you are

Father, I thank you for what You say concerning me. I believe Your word with all my heart and. with all my soul. I refuse to believe what my circumstances say. I refuse to believe what people say I stand on your word and therefore confess that I am what You say I am. And I am who You say I am.

I thank you for my victory over the evil one. I will live daily with the knowledge of the fact that I have overcome the evil one, in Jesus' Name, amen.

# #
46

YOU ARE A CHILD OF GOD

(1John 3:1)

"How great is the love the Father has lavished on us, that we should be called children of God! And that is what we are! The reason the world does not know us is that it did not know him."

There is a little song I like so much: it says *"I'm a child of God, hallelujah; I am born of God, hallelujah"*. It is a simple truth which when revealed to you will change your outlook of life. If you are a child of God it means God is ready to take care of all your needs. It means He knows you by name and calls you by name. It means He seeks your good and works for your good in everything. It means He seeks your interest in all things great or small. He is the best father you can ever think of. One who helps you in all you do. It means that He knows whatever is happening to you because He is all knowing. He will teach you all you need to know about Him and about life like any good father will do. You are a child of God if you have surrendered your life to Jesus. Nothing can change or contest with the fact. Not even your failures and weaknesses. This is an evidence of the demonstration of divine love, that you once lost and destined for everlasting destruction was rescued and made a child of the King of the universe. He says, *"Hearken unto me, O house of Jacob, and all the remnant of the house of Israel, which are borne by me from the belly, which are carried from the womb: And even to your old age I am he; and even to hoar hairs will I carry you: I have made, and I will bear; even I will carry, and will deliver you"* (Isaiah 46:3-4). He carried you from when you were born and He will carry you till your old age.

Proclaim what you are

Father, I thank you for what You say concerning me. I believe Your word with all my heart and. with all my soul. I refuse to believe what my circumstances say. I refuse to believe what people say I stand on your word and therefore confess that I am what You say I am. And I am who You say I am.

I rest assured of the fact that you have made me your child. I will enjoy all the privileges and live like a child of the Most High, in Jesus' Name, amen.

# #
47

GOD IS ABLE TO KEEP YOU FROM FALLING

(Jude 1:24; Psalm 55:22)

"To him who is able to keep you from falling and to present you before his glorious presence without fault and with great joy"
"Cast your cares on the LORD and he will sustain you; he will never let the righteous fall."

Do you still wonder if you will make it to the end? Are you still doubtful if you will fall or not? You must understand that God is able to keep you from falling and present you faultless to Himself. It is God who keeps you from falling. So do not be distracted any longer because of fear to fall. Focus on that which God has called you to do for Him and leave the matter of your safe arrival to Destiny-land in the hands of the One who has commissioned you.

From today you will no longer listen to the lies of the enemy that he will make you fall and miss heaven. He is not the one who called you or keeps you, so he cannot determine whether you will fall or not. The One who called you is God Almighty and He has said to keep you from falling. The Psalmist puts it more vividly. Cast all those cares and fear of falling on the Lord because He will never let the righteous fall. You just have to hold on to your righteousness.

Proclaim what you are

Father, I thank you for what You say concerning me. I believe Your word with all my heart and. with all my soul. I refuse to believe what my circumstances say. I refuse to believe what people say I stand on your word and therefore confess that I am what You say I am. And I am who You say I am.

I reject the fear of falling and cast all my cares on You Lord, knowing that You will sustain me on this journey to my destiny, in Jesus' Name.

# #
48

GOD GIVES YOU EVERYTHING FOR YOUR ENJOYMENT

(1 Timothy 6:17)

"Command those who are rich in this present world not to be arrogant nor to put their hope in wealth, which is so uncertain, but to put their hope in God, who richly provides us with everything for our enjoyment."

Many people are very miserable as Christians even though they have all they need. Their idea is that God does not want them to enjoy life here on earth. They wait the day they will enjoy life in heaven. I want you to know that God is interested in you enjoying your life here on earth. You don't have to appear miserable for you to serve God well. The reason He is providing you with all the blessing is that you should enjoy your life. He richly provides for you all you need so that you may enjoy your life in Him. Misery is not the emblem of consecration like some have made it to appear.

From today you will cease to be a miserable Christian in Jesus Name. You will begin enjoying your life as you serve the Lord. No more misery and unnecessary sorrow for you. God wants you to enjoy life. Do not mistake enjoying life with enjoying sinful pleasure. You can enjoy your life without compromising with sin. You can derive pleasure in everything you do in life. That is the way God wants you to live.

Proclaim what you are

Father, I thank you for what You say concerning me. I believe Your word with all my heart and. with all my soul. I refuse to believe what my circumstances say. I refuse to believe what people say I stand on your word and therefore confess that I am what You say I am. And I am who You say I am.

Misery shall not be part of my life, I will live joyfully and enjoyably, in Jesus' Name, amen.

# #
49

GOD HAS ASSIGNED YOUR PORTION

(Psalm 16:5-6)

"LORD, you have assigned me my portion and my cup; you have made my lot secure. The boundary lines have fallen for me in pleasant places; surely I have a delightful inheritance."

It means that God has kept for you your portion in a secure place. That which God has prepared for you is yours and he has made it secure. It will not get bad but you must reach out and receive it. Now just look at the list:
- He has assigned you your portion
- He has assigned you your cup
- He has made your lot secure
- The boundary lines have fallen for you in pleasant places
- Surely you have a delightful inheritance
  When the word surely is used it means there is absolutely no possibility of it being false or for it to fail. When God gives you a cup He causes it to run over. When God carved out your territory, He left out everything which is not pleasant and included all the pleasant things in your portion. That should cause you to rejoice and shout out. This should be your proclamation and declaration daily. When you get up in the morning thank the Lord for the pleasant and delightful things which will come

your way. Thank Him that what He has ordained for you shall come to you because your lot is secured.

Proclaim what you are

Father, I thank you for what You say concerning me. I believe Your word with all my heart and. with all my soul. I refuse to believe what my circumstances say. I refuse to believe what people say I stand on your word and therefore confess that I am what You say I am. And I am who You say I am.

I thank you Lord because my inheritance is a delightful one, thank you that mine is a pleasant land. Therefore, I reject and refuse to receive that which is not delightful and pleasant, in the Name of Jesus, amen.

# #
50

GOD WILL GUIDE YOU ALWAYS
(Psalm 32:8)

"I will instruct you and teach you in the way you should go; I will counsel you and watch over you."

God has promised to instruct (direct, lead, guide, show) and teach you on the way you should go. At every juncture of decision, the Lord is ready to tell you the best choice to make. Because He is all knowing you can trust His counsel. You must live daily, expecting the Lord to guide and lead you into that which he has ordained for you. I like the way the Living Bible puts that verse:

> You can live with all assurance to be guided by the Lord always and more so at moments of making consequential choices and decisions that will influence your life to a very great extend and even the life of others. That is why you must seek Him so that you can always make the best choice and receive the best in life.

Proclaim what you are

Father, I thank you for what You say concerning me. I believe Your word with all my heart and. with all my soul. I refuse to believe what my circumstances say. I refuse to believe what people say I stand on your word and therefore confess that I am what You say I am. And I am who You say I am.

I thank you for the availability of your guidance and leadership. I yield myself to your leadership and direction. Grand me to be flexible and malleable in your hands as I daily trust your guidance, in Jesus' Name, amen.

# #
51

GOD LOADS EACH DAY WITH BENEFITS FOR YOU

(Psalm 68:19, KJV)

"Blessed be the Lord, who daily loadeth us with benefits, even the God of our salvation. Selah."

As you get up each day, get up with great expectation to receive all the benefits which God has loaded into your day. When God prepares your day before it comes, He loads it with blessings for you. The sad thing is that many people spend their day but fail to enjoy these benefits because they often pass by them without entering them. What causes this is ignorance and lack of expectation.

Expect great things each day because God has so designed you day to be filled with benefits. Now that you know that there are benefits for you each day, let no day passes without you enjoying of those benefits. The ones you do not get hold of are lost because each new day comes with new benefits, different from the ones of the preceding day.

Proclaim what you are

Father, I thank you for what You say concerning me. I believe Your word with all my heart and. with all my soul. I refuse to believe what my circumstances say. I refuse to believe what people say I stand on your word and therefore confess that I am what You say I am. And I am who You say I am.

Thank you for the benefits of yesterday; those I got hold of and those I didn't get hold of. Thank you for the benefits of today. Lord I pray that I will get hold of each one you ordained for me. I refuse to pass by them. I confess that I will receive and enter into each one of them, in Jesus Name, amen.

# #
52

YOUR PAST SINS HAVE BEEN SEPARATED FAR FROM YOU

(Psalm 103:12)

"As far as the east is from the west, so far has he removed our transgressions from us."

Do you still brood over your past sins? Are there sins that appear to be so close to you that you can't live one moment without feeling their nearness? I want to let you that that nearness is just imaginary. When the Lord forgave your sins, He separated them from you as far as the east is from the west. Now if you can measure that distance then you know measure how far those sins are away from you.

When the Lord uses the east and the west here He is referring to the east and west ends of the universe. How great that distance is. Man has not yet discovered where the east of the universe is, neither have they measured where the west begins. So, from today henceforth know that your sins are not near you. When any past sin comes to your mind, command the demon who is feigning it to carry his property away.

The east has no contact with the west. Can you estimate the east of the universe from the west of it? That is how far God had effectively separated your sins from you. Not only your past since but also the sins you may ever commit will be separated from you when you genuinely repent of them. Somewhere in the Book, it is said about your God that, *"Who is a God like unto thee, that pardoneth iniquity, and passeth by the transgression of the remnant of his heritage? he retaineth not his anger for ever, because he delighteth in mercy. He will turn again, he will have compassion upon us; he will subdue our iniquities; and thou wilt cast all their sins into the depths of the sea"* (Micah 7:18-19). He doesn't just separate your sins from you as far as the eats is from the west, but also cast them into the sea of forgetfulness where he remembers them no more.

Proclaim what you are

Father, I thank you for what You say concerning me. I believe Your word with all my heart and. with all my soul. I refuse to believe what my circumstances say. I refuse to believe what people say I stand on your word and therefore confess that I am what You say I am. And I am who You say I am.

Thank you for separating me from my sins, I bear them no more and will bear them no more, in Jesus Name, amen.

# #
53

GOD WILL KEEP YOU FROM ALL HARM

(Psalm 121:7; Proverbs 12:21)

"The LORD will keep you from all harm-- he will watch over your life;"
"No harm befalls the righteous, but the wicked have their fill of trouble."

Do not live your life being in constant tension of the possibility of harm coming your way. You know God says in His word that He will not let your foot slip. He says He will save you from all the traps and snares of the enemy. And the truth is that the enemy puts thousands of the traps daily. I am quite sure he daily marvels at the fact that we do not get caught in such traps. Our heavenly Father keeps us safe. Whither it is danger in brought daylight or in the darkness of the night He has promised that none will touch us. The Lord is watching over your life and will keep you from all manner of harm.

When apparently bad things are happening around you, you must declare that they are not harm because your Father has promised that no harm will befall the righteous. He says, *"a thousand shall fall at thy side, and ten thousand at thy right hand; but it shall not come nigh thee"* (Psalm 91:7). Live in the consciousness that your father has made you harm-proof!

Proclaim what you are

Father, I thank you for what You say concerning me. I believe Your word with all my heart and. with all my soul. I refuse to believe what my circumstances say. I refuse to believe what people say I stand on your word and therefore confess that I am what You say I am. And I am who You say I am.

Father, from today I refuse to be concerned about the possibility of harm coming my way, I will live to follow your leading and be sure that no harm will ever come my way, because you have so decreed, in Jesus Name, amen.

# #
54

GOD KNEW YOU BEFORE YOU WERE BORN

(Psalm 139:15-16; Jeremiah 1:5)

"My frame was not hidden from you when I was made in the secret place. When I was woven together in the depths of the earth, your eyes saw my unformed body. All the days ordained for me were written in your book before one of them came to be."
"Before I formed you in the womb I knew you, before you were born I set you apart; I appointed you as a prophet to the nations."

Before you were ever born God foreknew you. He knew what you will look like at the age of 75. You do not need to make any self introduction. Before the sperm cell of your father came into contact with the egg cell of your mother, God determine which sperm cell was going to fertilize that egg. And in that race he favoured the sperm cell that would form you out of the million other sperm cells. He ensured that the process of development took place properly until you were born.

He knew the kind of hair you will have and He ordained for you what you must become in this world. His foreknowledge led Him to make adequate preparations for your life here on earth. With this knowledge, the best thing you can do for yourself is to live in utter transparency before God. You have been ordained for greatness from before your birth. God did not only know you but He ordained everything concerning you. It is your place to discover them and walk into each one of the great things that God has in store for you.

Proclaim what you are

Father, I thank you for what You say concerning me. I believe Your word with all my heart and. with all my soul. I refuse to believe what my circumstances say. I refuse to believe what people say I stand on your word and therefore confess that I am what You say I am. And I am who You say I am.

I am glad that you knew me and that you know my present and my future, my strengths and weaknesses. Help me live in total honesty and transparency before you, in Jesus' Name, amen.

# #
55

YOU ARE GOD'S SPECIAL HANDIWORK

(Psalm 139: 13-14)

"For you created my inmost being; you knit me together in my mother's womb. I praise you because I am fearfully and wonderfully made; your works are wonderful, I know that full well."

The Father took His time to knit you together. He arranged every part of your in its proper place. And when He had done so He acknowledged the wonder of what He had made before he decided when to post you through your mother's womb into planet earth for impact. The wonder and complexity that is in you continues to baffle scientist who take the pains to study humans. You see, God is a master potter, when He made you, if you were not what he wanted you to be, He would have remoulded you. You are not a mistake, you are God's masterpiece.

Next time you feel as though you were ugly and inferior, remind yourself that you are a masterpiece of God's. In deed that is what you are and will always be. God sees no mistake in you. You are a perfect work of God. Look your self in the mirror and shout that you are wonderfully made. Tell yourself you are God's masterpiece. Don't let no one deceive you by saying you are ugly. Tell the whole creation that you are beautiful, because that is what God says about you. Refuse and reject the lies of the enemy through what men have said in the negative.

Proclaim what you are

Father, I thank you for what You say concerning me. I believe Your word with all my heart and. with all my soul. I refuse to believe what my circumstances say. I refuse to believe what people say I stand on your word and therefore confess that I am what You say I am. And I am who You say I am.

I thank You Lord because I am your handiwork. I am a master piece of yours created for beauty and for glory, in Jesus' name, amen.

#56

GOD'S THOUGHTS ABOUT YOU ARE NUMEROUS AND PRECIOUS

(Psalm 139:17-18)

"How precious to me are your thoughts, O God! How vast is the sum of them! Were I to count them, they would outnumber the grains of sand. When I awake, I am still with you."

What you think concerning someone will determine your attitude towards that person and consequently, your actions will follow the line of your thoughts. The margin of that verse reads, *"How precious are your thoughts concerning me…"*

The Lord has just good and precious thoughts concerning you. In fact, may be if you have to live for three lifetimes you might not still be able to live out all the good things He thinks concerning you. When the devil whispers to you the fact that you are not loved by God, read out loud to him the verses above. And let him know that you know your Father's thoughts about you.

It is a privilege to have the King of the universe think about you, not just once in a while but, all the time. His thoughts about you are so vast that it will take you eternity to comprehend. Be relaxed and sure that your Father's thoughts concerning you are not only vast but they are precious. There is not a moment that you are not His mind.

Proclaim what you are

Father, I thank you for what You say concerning me. I believe Your word with all my heart and. with all my soul. I refuse to believe what my circumstances say. I refuse to believe what people say I stand on your word and therefore confess that I am what You say I am. And I am who You say I am.

I love Your thoughts concerning me, I am glad they are good and precious and vast. I will relax and be confident in the fact that your good thoughts for me are precious, in Jesus name, amen.

# #
57

GOD HAS GOOD PLANS FOR YOU

(Jeremiah 29:11)

"For I know the plans I have for you," declares the LORD, "plans to prosper you and not to harm you, plans to give you hope and a future."

The thoughts of God about you are not just some vain and baseless thoughts. They are thoughts which are tied to His plans for your life. I want you to notice here that plan here is in the plural. Therefore, God does not have only one plan for you but multiple plans which are adaptable in accordance with His infinite wisdom. So, if you think you have missed part of the plan for your life, do not fret, there are many of such plans which He will still unfold for you in accordance with His love and good thoughts towards you.

If you think you have missed some major aspect of the plan of the Lord for your life, trust Him to still bring out the best from your current situation. There is nothing impossible with God. He knows the end from the beginning so nothing is new with Him.

Proclaim what you are

Father, I thank you for what You say concerning me. I believe Your word with all my heart and. with all my soul. I refuse to believe what my circumstances say. I refuse to believe what people say

I stand on your word and therefore confess that I am what You say I am. And I am who You say I am.

I know your plans for my life will stand and not be thwarted. I believe you will prosper me in all I do, and in you my hope and future are secured, in Jesus Name, amen.

# #
58

GOD WILL NEVER LEAVE YOU NOR ABANDON YOU TILL YOU FULFIL YOUR DESTINY

(Genesis 28:15; 1Chronicles 28:20)

"I am with you and will watch over you wherever you go, and I will bring you back to this land. I will not leave you until I have done what I have promised you."
"David also said to Solomon his son, "Be strong and courageous, and do the work. Do not be afraid or discouraged, for the LORD God, my God, is with you. He will not fail you or forsake you until all the work for the service of the temple of the LORD is finished."

When the Lord met Jacob when he was fleeing to Aram, God told him that he will never leave him till He brings him to the place of promise. The place of God's promise for you is your destiny. For over a decade, I have continuously declared that I am immortal till I have accomplished God's purpose for my life.

When you know this the fear of death will leave you. It is the same thing David told his son Solomon when he was about taking over the throne of Israel. The truth is that God is not yet through with you because you are not yet through with His work, that is, what He created you for. God will never fail you nor forsake you. He is watching over you continuously to see His plan fulfilled in your life.

Proclaim what you are

Father, I thank you for what You say concerning me. I believe Your word with all my heart and. with all my soul. I refuse to believe what my circumstances say. I refuse to believe what people say I stand on your word and therefore confess that I am what You say I am. And I am who You say I am.

Thank you for the assurance of your presence with me. Thank you because you will never leave me nor forsake me. I will be strong and do the work you have given me knowing that you are with in through it all, in Jesus name, amen.

# #
59

NO WEAPON FORMED AGAINST YOU SHALL PROSPER

(Isaiah 54:17, KJV)

"No weapon that is formed against thee shall prosper; and every tongue that shall rise against thee in judgment thou shalt condemn. This is the heritage of the servants of the LORD, and their righteousness is of me, saith the LORD."

When a weapon is formed, it is specially design and assigned for a particular purpose. Now the enemy has several of such weapons he has designed against children of God. But the Lord has said no such weapons will prosper against you. The word 'prosper' here means to prevail. That is no weapon that the enemy has designed against you will accomplish its purpose. He may launch them against you if he will; they may even get to you if God so permits but the final outcome is that such weapons will never prevail against you for any and every reason. God will change the harmful effects of such weapons to you favour if He so permits the weapons to get to you. From today you should live knowing that you immune to all the weapons of the enemy. Launching them at you is like using a toy gun against an armoured vehicle in the battle field. God has made you resistant to all satan manufactured weapons.

Proclaim what you are

Father, I thank you for what You say concerning me. I believe Your word with all my heart and. with all my soul. I refuse to believe what my circumstances say. I refuse to believe what people say. I stand on your word and therefore confess that I am what You say I am. And I am who You say I am.

I will put on my whole armour of God daily knowing that I am in a war which I have already won. Thank you because with my armour on all the weapons of the enemy are destined to fail, in Jesus' Name, amen.

# #
60

NO WITCHCRAFT CAN WORK AGAINST YOU

(Numbers 23:23)

"There is no sorcery against Jacob, no divination against Israel. It will now be said of Jacob and of Israel, `See what God has done!"

We live in a society in which witchcraft is on the rise. In those days it was old mothers and fathers who were witches and wizards but, today it is the young beautiful girls and boys who are attacking people in the society. In fact, the old men are now very unsafe and helpless in the hands of this new generation of witches. All you need do to be attacked by them is to be ignorant and they will deal with you before you come to your senses.

Actually, the unbelievers are helpless but for you who are a child of God, all their schemes and devices will never do you anything because God has said there is no witchcraft, sorcery or divination against Israel, and we are the Israel of God. So, the next time you feel threatened by witchcraft, declare the above verse. It is fear and panic that creates an open door to the devil. When he gets you panicky he has access to you. But if you know that his agents can do nothing to you, you will maintain your boldness even in the city of witches and come out unscathed. So, from today stop running from the uncle or aunty or neighbour you consider a witch or wizard. They should run away from you.

Proclaim what you are

Father, I thank you for what You say concerning me. I believe Your word with all my heart and. with all my soul. I refuse to believe what my circumstances say. I refuse to believe what people say. I stand on your word and therefore confess that I am what You say I am. And I am who You say I am.

I am untouchable by the schemes of witches and wizards because my life is hid with Christ in God. When I appear witches and wizards will put to flight, their mutterings, incantations and spells will amount to nothing against me, in the Name of Jesus, amen.

# #
61

ALL WHO ATTACK YOU WILL SURRENDER TO YOU

(Isaiah 54:15; Isaiah 41:11)

"If anyone does attack you, it will not be my doing; whoever attacks you will surrender to you."
"All who rage against you will surely be ashamed and disgraced; those who oppose you will be as nothing and perish."

That is what the Lord has decreed on your behalf, that those who rage against you will be ashamed and disgraced. He has decreed that those who oppose you will be as nothing and perish. He has also decreed that those who attack you will surrender to you. You see the devil knows this very well, that is why he and his demons only use ignorant human agents to attack the saints, so that many of them will be reduced to nothing.

Satan hates to surrender, so he never comes himself. When you know this and the enemy knows that you know, he will steer clear of you and allow his ignorant agents to suffer the effects. That is what God has decreed about you.

Proclaim what you are

Father, I thank you for what You say concerning me. I believe Your word with all my heart and. with all my soul. I refuse to believe what my circumstances say. I refuse to believe what people say.

I stand on your word and therefore confess that I am what You say I am. And I am who You say I am.

Thank You Lord for my invincibility in You. That which You have decreed concerning me is what I choose to believe. Whether it be sickness or any such thing that dares to attack me will surrender to me in the Name of Jesus, amen.

# #
62

GOD WILL GIVE MEN IN EXCHANGE FOR YOU

(Isaiah 43:4)

"Since you are precious and honored in my sight, and because I love you, I will give men in exchange for you, and people in exchange for your life."

You are too precious in the eyes of the Lord to be victimised by the evil one. God will rather give a thousand unbelievers for your stead than allow you be victimised by the enemy. He did it for the Hebrew boys in Babylon, He did it for Daniel in the Persian kingdom, He did it for Peter when Herod tried to execute him.

And the truth is that God keeps on doing it today all across the globe to deliver His children from enemy attacks. God will do it for you anytime need be. You are a precious gem to God and he will give men in exchange to save you if that must happen. So, from today begin to live your life in confidence, void of all manner of fear.

Proclaim what you are

Father, I thank you for what You say concerning me. I believe Your word with all my heart and. with all my soul. I refuse to believe what my circumstances say. I refuse to believe what people say. I stand on your word and therefore confess that I am what You say I am. And I am who You say I am.

I refuse to live in any manner of fear because I am precious in Your sight o Lord. Thank you because you will give men in exchange for me anytime, anywhere there is need to. I will live unafraid of death or any kind of harm, in Jesus Name, amen.

# #
63

GOD WILL MAKE YOUR ROUGH PLACES SMOOTH

(Isaiah 42:16)

"I will lead the blind by ways they have not known, along unfamiliar paths I will guide them; I will turn the darkness into light before them and make the rough places smooth. These are the things I will do; I will not forsake them."

On the pathway to your destiny lie hills, mountains and several rough places. The Lord has promised to go ahead of you and make those rough places smooth. Without this there can be no way for you to make it to Destinyland. Do not be afraid of the obstacles that lie on your way when you are on the path to do what God has ordained for you to do. It is His responsibility to take care of the roadblocks, hills and mountains that obstruct your path.

So, from today face every difficulty with the knowledge that the Lord will level the mountains and make all rough places smooth for you. The ones He allows, He does so to teach you certain things. When you must have learned all He wanted, then the obstacle will be removed also. Each time you encounter hills, mountains, or rough places in your walk with God, invoke this promise of His in your favour. God responds to His word when appropriated by faith.

Proclaim what you are

Father, I thank you for what You say concerning me. I believe Your word with all my heart and. with all my soul. I refuse to believe what my circumstances say. I refuse to believe what people say. I stand on your word and therefore confess that I am what You say I am. And I am who You say I am.

I will face life and walk with You confident of the fact that you will always go ahead of me to take care of the obstacles. I will follow you wherever you lead, go wherever You send knowing You are aware and in control of every obstacle on my way, in Jesus' Name, amen.

# #
64

HE WILL GIVE YOU THE TREASURES OF DARKNESS

(Isaiah 45:2-3)

"I will go before you and will level the mountains; I will break down gates of bronze and cut through bars of iron. I will give you the treasures of darkness, riches stored in secret places, so that you may know that I am the LORD, the God of Israel, who summons you by name."

When man was deceived by the devil and the devil gained authority over the earth, he anticipated that man would one day seek to regain all his riches and so what satan did is that he quickly gathered the treasures of the earth and hid them in darkness where man would no longer have access to those riches and hidden treasures. However, because, no darkness is too dark for God, He can command those treasures to come to you, in fact He gives them to those who please Him and serve His purpose.

This promise was originally to Cyrus who was to rebuild the Temple. But you and I are also involved in rebuilding not just the temple but His kingdom. Many prophets of today have spoken about the wealth transfer that is soon coming, where the wealth of the heathen will be transferred to the saints. That which is yours which the enemy has hidden in darkness will be given you. It is time to ask the Lord for these treasures of darkness. They were yours but were stolen by the thief. He has been caught; it is time for him to restore what he stole.

Proclaim what you are

Father, I thank you for what You say concerning me. I believe Your word with all my heart and. with all my soul. I refuse to believe what my circumstances say. I refuse to believe what people say. I stand on your word and therefore confess that I am what You say I am. And I am who You say I am.

Thank You because what is mine that is hidden in darkness is coming to me, in Jesus' name, amen.

# #
65

WHAT GOD HAS PLANNED FOR YOU, NOTHING CAN THWART

(Isaiah 14:24,27)

"The LORD Almighty has sworn, "Surely, as I have planned, so it will be, and as I have purposed, so it will stand…For the LORD Almighty has purposed, and who can thwart him? His hand is stretched out, and who can turn it back?"

We said earlier that God has good plans for you in accordance with His eternal purpose for the whole universe. There is one who has also made plans for you; plans to ruin you and frustrate God's purpose for your life. The devil works tirelessly to see that many people forfeit or miss their destiny. But for you who have become a child of God all his attempts will be rendered null and void. Get up daily and use your authority to frustrate and nullify all the schemes of the evil one against you. In so doing you will ensure that God's plans for your life will come to pass.

Nothing, absolutely nothing can thwart what God in His sovereignty and omniscience has planned for you. Is it for your family life, your finances, your job, your spiritual life? As long as you live according to the rules prescribed in the word of God, you can live assured that nothing in the heavens, on earth or in the deepest recesses of hell will frustrate God's purpose for your life. Thank God daily for the fact that His will for your life will be accomplished. Thank Him for the fact that nothing can thwart His purpose for your life.

Proclaim what you are

Father, I thank you for what You say concerning me. I believe Your word with all my heart and. with all my soul. I refuse to believe what my circumstances say. I refuse to believe what people say. I stand on your word and therefore confess that I am what You say I am. And I am who You say I am.

Thank You because Your purposes for me will come to pass. All of hell let loose will not hinder any of it because You are with me like a mighty warrior, watching over each plan of Yours until everything is accomplished, in Jesus Name, amen.

# #
66

IT IS YOUR SEASON TO SHINE
(Isaiah 60:1; Philippians 2:15)

"Arise, shine, for your light has come, and the glory of the LORD rises upon you."
"so that you may become blameless and pure, children of God without fault in a crooked and depraved generation, in which you shine like stars in the universe."

The Lord commands you to arise now and shine like the light He has made of you. It is your time to shine in the ministry, it is your time to shine in your academics, it is your time to shine in the business you are doing. Obscurity for you is over! It is your time to be in the limelight. The Lord says His glory is rising upon you for all the earth to behold. You are meant to shine like a star. Stars shine brightest in the darkness night. The darkness that is increasing around you is just giving you an opportunity to shine brighter and further.

We are in the season of the glory of God rising on His church. And those of us on Zion are to shine with the glory that is rising upon us. It is time for darkness to flee from the light of God's presence that is reflecting on us. Get connected to the source of the glory so that you too can shine. Be a reflector of the glory into every area of darkness that is around you. Shine in your speech, your actions and in all that concerns you. It is your season to shine. God is taking you from the backyard of the desert to the frontline of notoriety. He is taking you from obscurity to the limelight, from peasantry to royalty. Declare and decree it that it is your season to shine.

Proclaim what you are

Father, I thank you for what You say concerning me. I believe Your word with all my heart and. with all my soul. I refuse to believe what my circumstances say. I refuse to believe what people say. I stand on your word and therefore confess that I am what You say I am. And I am who You say I am. I declare in accordance with your word that I am shining. Your glory is upon my life and reflects everywhere I go. I was made to shine like the stars. Nothing can cover my star any longer.

Now decree, "Oh star of... (insert your name) shine unhindered. The glory of the Lord is upon you."

# #
67

YOU ARE A FORTIFIED CITY

(Jeremiah 1:18; Jeremiah 15:20)

"Today I have made you a fortified city, an iron pillar and a bronze wall to stand against the whole land--against the kings of Judah, its officials, its priests and the people of the land."
"I will make you a wall to this people, a fortified wall of bronze; they will fight against you but will not overcome you, for I am with you to rescue and save you," declares the LORD."

I had come under serious threats from marine spirits and their human agents because I was carrying out deliverance on some of their agents. As I was meditating on the word of God, He suddenly gave me this revelation that ended all my fears. In fact, the day before, they came to me and said, *"leave us alone and we will leave you alone"*. The next morning the Lord led me to meditate on the above verses and that settled the problem once and for all. I declared it on the pulpit while preaching the following Sunday morning without any doubt.

You see, God has made you a fortified city of bronze. This means that the enemy cannot break into you until you open the gates to him. Keep your gates shut and no matter the siege ramp he builds outside, your walls will remain standing after all his materials for the siege work have been exhausted. They may attack but they are doomed to defeat. It is not you who made yourself a fortified city but it is God who made you so.

Proclaim what you are

Father, I thank you for what You say concerning me. I believe Your word with all my heart and. with all my soul. I refuse to believe what my circumstances say. I refuse to believe what people say. I stand on your word and therefore confess that I am what You say I am. And I am who You say I am.

Lord I will keep my wall in tact and allow no bridge in the wall. I will keep my gates shut and keep out the enemy permanently, in the Name of Jesus, amen.

#68

YOU ARE AN IRON PILLAR

(Jeremiah 1:18)

"Today I have made you a fortified city, an iron pillar and a bronze wall to stand against the whole land--against the kings of Judah, its officials, its priests and the people of the land."

The Lord says He has made you an iron pillar. An iron pillar cannot be moved; neither can it be bended nor broken. From today you will not be tossed around by the winds of the enemy's deceptions.

You will remain firm in the place God has put you, unmoved by the shakings of the enemy. If you believe that the Lord has made you an iron pillar I want you to proclaim it without fear or panic to the hearing of principalities and powers. When you know what you are, you act accordingly. You are not a reed to be blown and tossed by the wind whenever it likes. No, you are an iron pillar, planted and firm. From today you will live a stable life because you have known what you are.

Proclaim what you are

Father, I thank you for what You say concerning me. I believe Your word with all my heart and. with all my soul. I refuse to believe what my circumstances say. I refuse to believe what people say. I stand on your word and therefore confess that I am what You say I am. And I am who You say I am.

Thank you because You have made of me an iron pillar which cannot be moved or shaken. Thank you because I am a pillar planted in your house, in Jesus' Name, amen.

# #
69

YOU ARE A GOD

(Psalm 82:6; John 10:34)

"I said, 'You are "gods"; you are all sons of the Most High."

God declared that you are a god. You see the Psalmist said, indicating his amazement when he discovered what he was, *"you made him (man) a little lower than the heavenly beings (Elohim) and crowned him with glory and honour"* (Psalm 8:5 emphasis mine)

You see God made you just a little lower than Himself, that is why He said you are a god. From today you will stop living like a slave. You were made to live like a god. The Lord Jesus Himself reiterated the fact that you are a god. Your powers as a god were lost because of the fall. If you have professed Christ and are living according to godly principles, then your place as a god has been restored. That is why you can rule by decrees and speak things that are not as though they were.

Gods rule and exercise dominion. The Bible says God the almighty God has placed everything under your feet for you to rule and reign over. Begin to exercise your rule by proclaiming things into existence. Declare what you want to be in accordance with the Word of God and in rhythm with the moving of the Spirit of God and believe that it shall be so.

Proclaim what you are

Father, I thank you for what You say concerning me. I believe Your word with all my heart and. with all my soul. I refuse to believe what my circumstances say. I refuse to believe what people say. I stand on your word and therefore confess that I am what You say I am. And I am who You say I am.

I will exercise my dominion by being sensitive to your word and the moving of Your Spirit, in Jesus Name, amen.

# #
70

YOU ARE THE APPLE OF GOD'S EYE

(Zechariah 2:8)

"For this is what the LORD Almighty says: "After he has honored me and has sent me against the nations that have plundered you-- for whoever touches you touches the apple of his eye".

The apple of one's eye is the most sensitive part the reflex mechanism of the body will protect in case of the most subtle intruder. The eyelid closes rapidly against any from of attack on the pupil. So, when God says you are the apple of His eye, this means He will not allow any harm to come near you. It means you are an integral and precious element in His body. You can not be touched without God being affected.

Any one who touches you for any and every reason comes under wrath. That is why David could pray and say, *"Keep me as the apple of your eye"* (Psalm 17:8a). You can get up each morning and echo that prayer to God, for in deed you are the apple of God's eye.

Proclaim what you are

Father, I thank you for what You say concerning me. I believe Your word with all my heart and. with all my soul. I refuse to believe what my circumstances say. I refuse to believe what people say. I stand on your word and therefore confess that I am what You say I am. And I am who You say I am.

Keep me Lord, as the apple of your eye today, tomorrow, forever. I will live with the consciousness that I am the apple of your eye, in Jesus' Name, amen.

# #
71

YOU ARE ENGRAVED ON THE PALMS OF GOD'S HANDS

(Isaiah 49:16)

"See, I have engraved you on the palms of my hands; your walls are ever before me."

When something has been engraved on an object, it is impossible to erase that inscription without destroying the object. If it were a normal writing, it could be wiped without destroying the object. God did not just write you on some piece of paper, He did not just paint you somewhere; He engraved you on the palms of His hands. This means you are on both palms of the hands of God. When He looks at His right hand, He sees you there. When He looks at the left hand, He sees you there. In other words, you are permanently seen by God all the times of the day.

God will never forget you. You are always before the Lord, whatever you are passing through, He is aware. Before anything reaches you, He sees it already. In fact, God is daily aware of you more than you are aware of yourself. Nothing can wipe you from the palms of the Lord. You were not just written but engraved permanently on the palms of the Lord. That should give you all the confidence you need to face the most uncertain of circumstances. God doesn't have to look through the clouds to see you. If there is one part of the body that one sees often, it is the palm of one's hand. Whatever is in the palm is seen continuously. God has you in sight.

Proclaim what you are

Father, I thank you for what You say concerning me. I believe Your word with all my heart and with all my soul. I refuse to believe what my circumstances say. I refuse to believe what people say. I stand on your word and therefore confess that I am what You say I am. And I am who You say I am.

Lord, You see me daily. I am never out of your sight. Thank you that you see all that comes my way before they happen, in Jesus' Name, amen.

# #
72

YOU ARE A SPIRITUAL IMPERIALIST

(Deuteronomy 11:24)

"Every place where you set your foot will be yours: Your territory will extend from the desert to Lebanon, and from the Euphrates River to the western sea."

You were designed to be a spiritual imperialist, possessing every place your foot steps on. You see the enemy deceived our fore fathers and stole their territory. He now makes claim to so many places. But you know what? In these last days, God has designated you and I to repossess all what rightfully belongs to us and has made of us imperialist, dispossessing the enemy of the places he claims ownership. God has made it possible for you to extend your spiritual domain to whatever extend you want if only you will be able to maintain order there and keep the spiritual atmosphere under control. Do not allow your domain to be colonised by the devil and his cohorts any more.

Determine how large you want your domain to be and set out to possess that which is rightfully yours. The devil is a thief; do not allow him to continue to occupy stolen territory that belongs to you. Every place means all but none. You must see yourself as an imperialist, driving out the enemy and taking possession of the land. Blessed be the name of the Lord, who has made it thus for you and me. You may write out new territories to possess and set out to possess them. Imperialists are unstoppable. See yourself as one who will be stopped by nothing. Your God is unstoppable and so He has made you unstoppable.

Proclaim what you are

Father, I thank you for what You say concerning me. I believe Your word with all my heart and. with all my soul. I refuse to believe what my circumstances say. I refuse to believe what people say. I stand on your word and therefore confess that I am what You say I am. And I am who You say I am.

I will set out for new territories, I refuse to be stopped by anything. I am reaching out for all that is mine, every occupied territory must be repossessed, and I am setting out for them, in Jesus' name, amen.

# #
73

YOU ARE A TERROR TO THE DEVIL

(Deuteronomy 11:25)

"No man will be able to stand against you. The LORD your God, as he promised you, will put the terror and fear of you on the whole land, wherever you go."

When you live according to divine principles and values, when your life is saturated with the presence of the Most High, you become a terror to the enemy and his cohorts. The presence of God in you and on you causes the enemy to retreat on your approach. He flees helter-skelter when he beholds the blazing fire of the Holy Ghost that surrounds the one who carries the anointing of God. In order for you to maintain your capacity to be a terror to the enemy, you must live in holiness, purity, and consciousness of the fact that God has made you a terror to satan.

You know, with spiritual matters, it is your heart knowledge which determines the effect your life produces on your environment. If you do not know who you are, creation will not respect nor respond to that which it will automatically respond to if only you had known who you are. In fact, knowledge is power, and commands respect and obedience.

The one who knows is known and feared by all of hell. It is for that reason the devil does all to keep people from knowing the truth. But you have known the truth today and may it set you free from all fear of the evil one. Just like the world today is afraid of terrorists, so the enemy kingdom is afraid of you, I wish you knew this earlier. But now that you know this, do not be afraid of the petty threats of the devil. Keep the Holy presence of the Most High with you and you will terrorize the enemy camp.

Proclaim what you are

Father, I thank you for what You say concerning me. I believe Your word with all my heart and. with all my soul. I refuse to believe what my circumstances say. I refuse to believe what people say. I stand on your word and therefore confess that I am what You say I am. And I am who You say I am.

By my obedience I will terrorize the enemy, by my prayers and fasting I will terrorize his camp. Because I am a carrier of the Divine presence I will advance boldly into all that You have ordained for me, in Jesus' Name, amen

# #
74

YOU ARE SURROUNDED WITH FAVOUR

(Psalm 5:12)

"For surely, O LORD, you bless the righteous; you surround them with your favor as with a shield."

If you are a child of God, blood-bought and blood-washed, then Christ Jesus has become your righteousness from God, and therefore you are a righteous. The Bible says God surrounds the righteous with favour as with a shield. This means for anything to reach you, it must first of all go through the shield of favour. Favour acts as a filter and blocks all harmful components from coming to you. When you know that you are surrounded by favour, you live at peace and in confidence. You become unafraid of the deceitful scheming of men.

You know that all things that reach you come in accordance with the favour that surrounds you and thus you live expecting only good things to come your way. The suffering that comes to you is favour proven. The trials which come to you are favour proven. The disappointments which come to you are favour proven. From today live and act like one who knows he or she is shielded by the favour of the Lord. Knowledge of divine favour in your life will change your beliefs and attitude to life for the better and will enhance your performance and productivity even in the face of adversity.

Proclaim what you are

Father, I thank you for what You say concerning me. I believe Your word with all my heart and. with all my soul. I refuse to believe what my circumstances say. I refuse to believe what people say. I stand on your word and therefore confess that I am what You say I am. And I am who You say I am.

Thank You for Your favour that surrounds me. Lord I believe that nothing reaches me without going through this shied of favour to my front, to my back, to my left, to my right, above me and below me. I am soaked in Divine favour and I will live in this consciousness, in the name of Jesus, amen.

# #
75

YOU ARE MORE THAN A CONQUEROR
(Romans 8:37)

"No, in all these things we are more than conquerors through him who loved us."

To conquer means to overcome, surmount, triumph over, defeat, beat, overpower or get the better of. A conqueror is one who conquers. For God to say you are more than a conqueror, meaning you are more than a defeater, vanquisher, subjugator, or captor. You have the capacity to take captive everything that opposes your upward call. The last thing a conqueror will do is give up in the face of adversity. In fact, giving up or retreating is not in the vocabulary of a conqueror. And since you are more than a conqueror from today you will never retreat or give in to your enemy.

I know that all that which has troubled you until now is in trouble because you shall begin to act like what God has made you- more than a conqueror. Are there some things you have not conquered? It is time to rise up as the *"more than conqueror"* you are and conquer. Be reminded that you are more than a conqueror only in God who loved you. That is why sensitivity to His moves is essential.

Proclaim what you are

Father, I thank you for what You say concerning me. I believe Your word with all my heart and. with all my soul. I refuse to

believe what my circumstances say. I refuse to believe what people say. I stand on your word and therefore confess that I am what You say I am. And I am who You say I am. I will face every battle in life knowing you have made me more than a conqueror, in Jesus' Name, amen.

# #
76

YOU CAN LOVE EVERYBODY

(Romans 5:5)

"And hope does not disappoint us, because God has poured out his love into our hearts by the Holy Spirit, whom he has given us."

As a believer, it is impossible for you to hate anyone. If any feeling of hatred should arise in you towards anybody, then it is not from you. It has a strange origin. This might be from an evil spirit of hate residing in you or operating from without you. In such a case you have to tell yourself and declare the fact that you love that person.

It is the Holy Spirit Himself who has shed the love of God in your heart and therefore has given you the capacity to love everybody. Do not listen to the lies of the enemy that you hate anyone. You become guilty when you concur with the enemy that you hate that person. Hatred is not your product. Reject it and send it back to its source. Confess love and look for opportunities to show and practise love.

Proclaim what you are

Father, I thank you for what You say concerning me. I believe Your word with all my heart and. with all my soul. I refuse to believe what my circumstances say. I refuse to believe what people say. I stand on your word and therefore confess that I am what You say I am. And I am who You say I am.

I have the capacity to love everybody because the love of God has been poured into my heart abundantly. I release myself to be an agent of love to all who come my way. May people taste of Your love as they come in contact with me, in Jesus' Name, amen.

# #
77

YOU HAVE OVERCOME THE WORLD

(1 John 5:4)

"For everyone born of God overcomes the world. This is the victory that has overcome the world, even our faith."

The Lord Jesus told his disciples, *"In this world you will have trouble. But take heart! I have overcome the world"* (John 16:23 b&c). That was before He died and rose again. But now He says, anyone born of God overcomes the world. Are you a child of God? Then you have faith. And because you have faith, you have overcome the world. Its attractions, offers, promises, challenges, passions, values and all what this world has and is made of. In my book *"Child of God"* I wrote extensively on the world; the different aspects that make up the world system and how you can deal with them. Do well to get a copy and read it so as to know what makes you a child of God and how you can live effectively.

Proclaim what you are

Father, I thank you for what You say concerning me. I believe Your word with all my heart and. with all my soul. I refuse to believe what my circumstances say. I refuse to believe what people say. I stand on your word and therefore confess that I am what You say I am. And I am who You say I am.

# #
78

YOU HAVE BEEN HEALED

(1Peter 2:24)

"He himself bore our sins in his body on the tree, so that we might die to sins and live for righteousness; by his wounds you have been healed."

The Lord Jesus Christ has paid for our healing, total and complete healing. Nothing has the right to afflict you for any reason. In my book, *"Abundant Life"* I wrote extensively on the abundant healing of a believer. You will do well to get and read. Knowledge is power!

Proclaim what you are

Father, I thank you for what You say concerning me. I believe Your word with all my heart and. with all my soul. I refuse to believe what my circumstances say. I refuse to believe what people say. I stand on your word and therefore confess that I am what You say I am. And I am who You say I am.

Lord, I enter into my inheritance of health this day. I renounce every sickness and disease in my body for by the wounds of the Lord Jesus Christ I am healed, in Jesus' Name, amen.

# #
79

YOU ARE A CHILD OF PROMISE

(Galatians 4:28)

"Now you, brothers, like Isaac, are children of promise."

You are carrying on you the promise of the Father. You are a child of promise just like Isaac was to his father Abraham. It means that your slaves have no write to share in your inheritance. You cannot allow yourself to be treated by the devil like an ordinary person. Children of promise are children of hope, favour and a future that is blessed and sealed with the love of God. As a child of promise you are meant to prosper even in the midst of famine like Isaac did. You are meant to be a match for entire communities by your hard work, wisdom and success.

Because Isaac was a child of promise he could not be killed because God's purposes for future generations were tied to him. Listen, if you allow this truth to sink into the inside of you, your confidence as you face the hurdles of life will be overwhelming. There is divine promise written all over you. The enemy knows it but if he knows that you are not aware of that he will try to use it to his advantage. Remember ignorance is the greatest disservice you can do yourself.

Proclaim what you are

Father, I thank you for what You say concerning me. I believe Your word with all my heart and. with all my soul. I refuse to be-

lieve what my circumstances say. I refuse to believe what people say. I stand on your word and therefore confess that I am what You say I am. And I am who You say I am.

Thank You for Your promise written all over my life. Just as no promise of yours can fail so will I fulfil my destiny. All that you have ordained for me will come to pass, each at the right time, in Jesus Name, amen.

# #
80

YOU HAVE A READY SOURCE OF HELP
(Hebrews 4:16)

"Let us then approach the throne of grace with confidence, so that we may receive mercy and find grace to help us in our time of need."

There is ready help available for you from the throne of grace. The Lord invites you to His Throne, so as to find mercy and grace that will provide you the necessary help when you are in need. Many people do not tap from this source of help because they do not draw near the source. You have a source of emotional, psychological, moral, physical, social, and above all spiritual help from which you can tap.

As long as you are in this tabernacle of clay, there are moments when you shall be too weak to fight. At such moments just connect, by approaching the Throne of grace, to your source of help. Help is nearer you each time than you are aware of. Just a short phrase of *"help me Lord"*, mixed with faith can release as many angels as are needed for intervention on your behalf.

As you live daily, implore the help of the Lord not only in times of emergency but in everything you do. The throne of grace is within your reach, child of destiny. Let it be a place you constantly visit. Grace is divine enabling to do what you will otherwise not be able to do. So, you have God's abilities put within your reach for daily living, exploit it.

Proclaim what you are

Father, I thank you for what You say concerning me. I believe Your word with all my heart and. with all my soul. I refuse to believe what my circumstances say. I refuse to believe what people say. I stand on your word and therefore confess that I am what You say I am. And I am who You say I am.

Thank You my Father, because You are an ever-present source of help. I will draw near Your throne of grace in prayer and worship, and through the meditations of my heart, In Jesus' Name, amen.

# #
81

YOU WERE MADE IN THE IMAGE OF GOD
(Genesis 1:27)

"So God created man in his own image, in the image of God he created him; male and female he created them."

Do you know why satan hates mankind with such intense hatred? It is because each time he looks at man he sees the creator in man. Man was made like God. Even after the fall the image is still there, what were destroyed were the God-given potentials. Because satan cannot do anything to God he attempts to vent his anger on the image of God, which is man. He derives his satisfaction from afflicting God's beloved human race.

Did you see the way the Iraqis trampled the statue of Saddam after his fall? They were not trampling on the real man but they derived pleasure in what they did because they trampled on his image. It is the same pleasure the maniacs of evil driven out of the Kingdom of Light in disgrace are deriving in afflicting mankind. But thanks be to God, who through Christ Jesus has turned the tables and given us the upper hand, now we can punish the devil by the power of the Holy Ghost.

You are in the image of God. Do not listen any more to the lies of the evil one that are meant to belittle you and make you think you are a nobody. Not only the image of God in you has been enhanced but the potentials of God in you have also been restored by the redemption provided for in Christ Jesus.

Proclaim what you are

Father, I thank you for what You say concerning me. I believe Your word with all my heart and. with all my soul. I refuse to believe what my circumstances say. I refuse to believe what people say. I stand on your word and therefore confess that I am what You say I am. And I am who You say I am.

Thank You Lord for making me in your image and placing in me Your own potentials. I will explore all You have placed in me to the fullest by the enabling of Your Spirit, in Jesus' Name, amen.

# #
82

YOU WERE FASHIONED TO BE IN CONTROL

(Genesis 1:28; Psalm 8:3-8)

"God blessed them and said to them, "Be fruitful and increase in number; fill the earth and subdue it. Rule over the fish of the sea and the birds of the air and over every living creature that moves on the ground."
"When I consider your heavens, the work of your fingers, the moon and the stars, which you have set in place, what is man that you are mindful of him, the son of man that you care for him? You made him a little lower than the heavenly beings and crowned him with glory and honor."

When God made you, He built you with the intention that you should be in control, that is, He made you with the capacity to lead, dominate, and rule the rest of creation on the earth. Whether it be creatures on the lower lithosphere and asthenosphere or in the upper troposphere, stratosphere, mesosphere or thermosphere. As long as it is in the earth's domain, God made you with the inherent ability to be in control. It is for this reason the normal man will not want to be controlled because he was originally designed to be in control and not be under control. From today do not see yourself any longer as one who can never lead. In his book, *"becoming a leader"* Dr Myles Monroe wrote: *"God created all of us to rule, govern, control and influence the earth. He created all of us to lead... you were never charted to be dominated."*

However, there are people who enjoy being dominated and confuse it for being submissive. In doing so they fail to fine a full expression of that which God has put in them. What you need in life is guidance and counsel and not control. In fact, to properly be in control you do need mature guidance and counsel of others.

Learn to be in control of your actions, words, thoughts etc. Learn to be in control of circumstances which come your way even when unanticipated. Never allow yourself to lose control of anything from this day henceforth. God fashioned you to be in control and exercise dominion. The Lord Jesus Christ came to restore your ability to have things under control.

Proclaim what you are

Father, I thank you for what You say concerning me. I believe Your word with all my heart and. with all my soul. I refuse to believe what my circumstances say. I refuse to believe what people say. I stand on your word and therefore confess that I am what You say I am. And I am who You say I am.

# #
83

YOU ARE A CHILD OF DESTINY

(Romans 8:30; Ephesians 1:11)

"And those he predestined, he also called; those he called, he also justified; those he justified, he also glorified."
"In him we were also chosen, having been predestined according to the plan of him who works out everything in conformity with the purpose of his will."

God predetermined your purpose on earth. He designed and made you with a particular purpose in mind for you to accomplish. It is this predetermined purpose of God's concerning you that is called destiny. In fact, He Himself talks of bringing you to an expected end. That expected end is your destiny. That is why He works out everything in your life to conform to His predetermined plan and purpose.

You are not a child of circumstance so as to live according to chances. No! Everything about you is written. There is a blueprint that God is following for your life. You can trust Him! The psalmist said, *"All the days ordained for me were written in your book before one of them came to be"* (Psalm 139: 16b). Do not live anymore by chance, fine out your destiny and fulfil it. You can read my book, *"Fulfilling your Destiny"*. You must understand that whatever comes your way, God works it out in conformity to the purpose of His will for your life.

Proclaim what you are

Father, I thank you for what You say concerning me. I believe Your word with all my heart and. with all my soul. I refuse to believe what my circumstances say. I refuse to believe what people say. I stand on your word and therefore confess that I am what You say I am. And I am who You say I am.

Lord, I will pursue nothing else but what you wrote concerning me in Your book. I give you the permission Lord to block whatever is not part of Your purpose for me and to open the doors that will lead me to fulfilling my destiny in you, in Jesus' Name, amen.

# #
84

GOD HAS MADE YOU STORM AND FLAME RESISTANT

(Isaiah 43:2)

"When you pass through the waters, I will be with you; and when you pass through the rivers, they will not sweep over you. When you walk through the fire, you will not be burned; the flames will not set you ablaze."

Have you ever used a wristwatch on which was inscribed *"water resistant"*? How did you act when you came in contact with water while putting on such a watch? In fact, you cared less if the watch fell into water. You could even bathe or swim with the watch on because you were confident that water will not affect the functioning of the watch. Now that is what God has done for you! However, He made you both water and flame resistant.

The raging waters of the enemy, when they come against you will not affect you. The flames of affliction will not affect your life in anyway. Though you may go through the waters and fires of life, you will come out unscathed, without any hair on your body being singed. In fact, they only come to help take away any dirt or impurity that might have been in you. From today you shall cease to be afraid of storms. The fire that comes your way comes to burn away the dross from your life. The water you go through is meant to take away any filth that may have rubbed on you. You are water and flame resistant.

Proclaim what you are

Father, I thank you for what You say concerning me. I believe Your word with all my heart and. with all my soul. I refuse to believe what my circumstances say. I refuse to believe what people say. I stand on your word and therefore confess that I am what You say I am. And I am who You say I am.

Thank you because every fire I go through is for the purpose of purification and cleansing. Thank You for being committed to purge away every dross and impurity from my life, in Jesus' Name, amen.

# #
85

YOU ARE GOD'S TREASURED POSSESSION
(Psalm 135:4; Ephesians 3:6)

"For the LORD has chosen Jacob to be his own, Israel to be his treasured possession."
"This mystery is that through the gospel the Gentiles are heirs together with Israel, members together of one body, and sharers together in the promise in Christ Jesus."

You see, because you are in Christ Jesus, you have become a sharer of all the promises God gave to Israel. One of such promise was that Israel was going to be His treasured possession among all the nations of the earth (Exodus 19:5) and the psalmist confirms it in the above psalm quoted. So, you should know that God has chosen you to be His treasured possession. He treats you and keeps you like anyone will treat and keep a treasure. You have a special value in the sight of the Almighty God.

Those who look low on you or treat you with contempt do not know your worth. They do not know your worth because they do not matter. The One who matters most in your life says you are a treasured possession of His. It is the value He gives you that counts. Anyone who wants to matter in your life should accept the value God has given you or he or she is not worth your attention.

Proclaim what you are

Father, I thank you for what You say concerning me. I believe Your word with all my heart and. with all my soul. I refuse to believe what my circumstances say. I refuse to believe what people say. I stand on your word and therefore confess that I am what You say I am. And I am who You say I am.

I will continue to walk in obedience, sanctified and consecrated totally to you. Thank You for making me a treasured possession of Yours. It is a privilege Lord, and I stand in awe of You for what You have made of me, in Jesus Name, amen.

# #
86

YOUR FUTURE IS BRIGHTER THAN YOUR PRESENT

(Proverbs 4:18)

"The path of the righteous is like the first gleam of dawn, shining ever brighter till the full light of day."

No matter how delighted you are in your present, there are greater prospects for your future. No matter how rich you are today, if you are a righteous then your future will be richer. No matter how successful you have been all this while your future is pack loaded with more trilling stories of success. God so designed that the path of the righteous should go brighter and brighter as he walks on it.

As long as you remain on the path to your destiny, things are bound to get better for you, financially, emotionally, socially and otherwise. Anything that seems contrary is just a gateway to the ultimate purpose of making life better for you. You have brighter days ahead of you than you can imagine. Just keep walking on your God-ordained lane. Anytime things appear darker than they were previously, then it should ring a bell that something isn't going well. Expect things to get brighter and better as you walk the path of your destiny.

Proclaim what you are

Father, I thank you for what You say concerning me. I believe Your word with all my heart and. with all my soul. I refuse to believe what my circumstances say. I refuse to believe what people say.

I stand on your word and therefore confess that I am what You say I am. And I am who You say I am.

I confess that my days are getting better, brighter, richer. My path is getting clearer each passing day. My coast is getting bigger, I am rising higher, growing stronger, wiser, more compassionate each and every day, in Jesus Name, amen.

# #
87

GOODNESS AND MERCY HAVE BEEN ASSIGNED TO YOU

(Psalm 23:6)

"Surely goodness and mercy will follow me all the days of my life, and I will dwell in the house of the LORD forever."

You have two faithful compassions to accompany you with the blessings of the Lord. One is goodness and the other is mercy. Goodness brings you all the good things that God has ordained to come your way and converts the bad things that satan sends your way to work for your good. Mercy is there to ensure that you days are loaded with God's mercy, that even before the most cruel of your enemies mercy will always prevail on your behalf.

Do you see the word *"surely"* in that verse? It means that with all certainty, without any possibility of failure, goodness and mercy have been assigned to you always. Live daily in the goodness the Lord has assigned to you. Tap into God's mercy following you and let it flow out to others. When ever you notice anything that doesn't look like it's coming from goodness or mercy coming after you, address it and tell it, it is following the wrong person, it certainly has missed its way. Confess the truth, live it, experience it and pass it unto others. Anything that is not coming from these two has to right to follow you. Daily blind the eyes of all illegal followers and create room for the goodness and mercy ordained of the Lord to follow you without hindrance.

Proclaim what you are

Father, I thank you for what You say concerning me. I believe Your word with all my heart and. with all my soul. I refuse to believe what my circumstances say. I refuse to believe what people say. I stand on your word and therefore confess that I am what You say I am. And I am who You say I am.

You have assigned Your goodness and Your mercy to follow me all the days of my life. Lord I reject whatever is following me which is not associated with or released by Your goodness and mercy. I will experience Your goodness and Your mercy everywhere I go and in whatever I do, in Jesus' Name, amen.

# #
88

YOU HAVE THE POWER TO SHAPE YOUR DESTINY

(Numbers 14:28)

"So tell them, 'As surely as I live, declares the LORD, I will do to you the very things I heard you say'"

The Bible says there is tremendous power to give life or cause death in the tongue of any human. More so, for believers whose words have creative power, this is a more serious truth. In the above verse God expresses the fact that He will do to us the very things we utter, whether consciously or unconsciously. By your declarations, pronouncements and utterances you can shape your destiny by declaring the things which God has said about you.

There are too many people who are the architects of their own misfortune because of the things they often say. From today you must understand that your destiny is in your mouth. You must take sides with God and declare the things He has declared about you in His word. When you do that, you are shaping your destiny in accordance with God's will for you. It is the more reason you must fill your heart with the word of God. *"Let the words of Christ dwell in you richly"* so that in times of emergency it will be released whether consciously or unconsciously.

As you speak the word of God from your heart it goes out to work for you. Your boss, spouse, relative or government is not what is responsible for where you are. Your words have paved the way for where you are right now and only your words can pave the way out for you. Do you want a change in circumstances? Then begin to declare and proclaim what the word of God says about you.

Proclaim what you are

Father, I thank you for what You say concerning me. I believe Your word with all my heart and. with all my soul. I refuse to believe what my circumstances say. I refuse to believe what people say. I stand on your word and therefore confess that I am what You say I am. And I am who You say I am.

Forgive me Lord, for all the negative words which have brought me to my present situation. I decide to declare just what you say about me. From today I will take charge of my destiny and letting my heart be filled with Your words so my mouth will declare it, in Jesus' Name, amen.

89

THERE ARE ANGELS ALL AROUND YOU

(Psalm 34:7; Hebrews 1:14)

"The angel of the LORD encamps around those who fear him, and he delivers them."
"Are not all angels ministering spirits sent to serve those who will inherit salvation?"

Angels are your faithful companions assigned to assist and protect you in the daily affairs of life. You can use them in warfare. They encamp around you to protect you and receive orders from you in what domain you want them to intervene in your daily life. Many of us fail to make use of this God – given resource for daily living. They will not act until you or the Father gives them orders. They are sent to serve you and so they wait on you for appropriate instructions to carry out on your behalf.

From today begin to make use of your angels. You are privileged to have the Father assign them to you, do not waste this wonderful resource placed at your service by the Father. Personally, I have seen angels work on my behalf on so many occasions. I have made them my partners in ministry, especially when I am carrying out deliverance. I have seen them bring very fast results. They are there for you. They do not have limitations like we do. They have access to places you will never go in this life.

Proclaim what you are

Father, I thank you for what You say concerning me. I believe Your word with all my heart and. with all my soul. I refuse to believe what my circumstances say. I refuse to believe what people say. I stand on your word and therefore confess that I am what You say I am. And I am who You say I am.

Lord, I will call upon You for angelic interventions. I will command the angels to go work in my favour. I will make use of them in spiritual warfare. Thank you for placing them at my command, in Jesus' Name, amen.

# #
90

YOU ARE A LIVING FLAME OF FIRE
(Hebrews 1:7)

"In speaking of the angels he says," He makes his angels winds, his servants flames of fire."

The God whom you serve is a consuming fire, and because you are His offspring He has made of you a living flame of fire. When fire burns on intent, it does so either to destroy that which is unwanted or to produce useful energy. God has made you a flame of fire so that you will burn away the works of the enemy in your life and in your environment. You are a flame of fire so that from you, others can catch the flame of devotion and service to your God. But remember that fire can be put off, so you must guard against anything that can put off the flame in you.

There are times when in ministering to people they have felt as though touched by fire. When demons see you, they see fire. This happens when you activate the flame of fire around you by faith. Several times I have asked the Lord to let me appear as flames of fire in the spirit realm. In this way strange things steer clear. When you are flames of fire whatever approaches you is burned. In fact, evil things stay far from you because of fear of being consumed.

Proclaim what you are

Father, I thank you for what You say concerning me. I believe Your word with all my heart and. with all my soul. I refuse to believe what my circumstances say. I refuse to believe what people say. I stand on your word and therefore confess that I am what You say I am. And I am who You say I am.

I will maintain my flame and protect it from all fire extinguishers. I will fuel the fire I am to burn increasingly by the oil of Your presence, in Jesus' name, amen.

# #
91

YOU ARE AN HEIR OF THE FATHER

(Romans 8:16-17)

"The Spirit himself testifies with our spirit that we are God's children. Now if we are children, then we are heirs--heirs of God and co-heirs with Christ, if indeed we share in his sufferings in order that we may also share in his glory."

Because you are an heir of the Father, it means that all that the Father owns is yours. You have a birth right to whatever belongs to your Father no matter where it is located. And you know what? The Bible says *"the earth is the Lord's and everything in it"* (Psalm 24:1a). Elsewhere it is said the cattle on a thousand hills are all His, that all the silver and gold there is in this world belongs to God.

You are an heir to His power and authority. You are an heir to His nature and character. The primary thing that an heir inherits is not the property of the one he is heir to but the character of the person. See yourself and live daily as an heir of the Father. The silver and gold, power and authority, love and faithfulness are all yours to possess. Allow nothing, absolutely nothing to cheat you of all that belongs to you.

Proclaim what you are

Father, I thank you for what You say concerning me. I believe Your word with all my heart and. with all my soul. I refuse to

believe what my circumstances say. I refuse to believe what people say. I stand on your word and therefore confess that I am what You say I am. And I am who You say I am.

Thank You for giving me access to possess all that is of You and all that is Yours. By faith Lord I appropriate all that is mine as an heir to the Father; the silver and gold, riches and honor, power and authority, love and faithfulness; Lord, just everything that is You or is of You, in Jesus' Name, amen.

# #
92

YOU HAVE RESURRECTION POWER IN YOU

(Ephesians 1:19-20)

"And his incomparably great power for us who believe. That power is like the working of his mighty strength, which he exerted in Christ when he raised him from the dead and seated him at his right hand in the heavenly realms"

The Bible says the kind of power that is in us the believers is that same power which God exerted mightily when He raised Christ and seated Him in the heavenly places. It is that same power you are carrying. It is just that we have all learned only to varying and limited degrees of how to release the power in us. The secret lies in having a revelation of the power and on how to release it. When I first discovered this truth, it greatly enhanced the degree of power in my deliverance sessions. I discovered that this same power is locked up in me and so by faith I set out to use it to bring deliverance to captives.

I want to tell you the truth that the difference in anointing levels of believers just lies in the fact that some have mastered the secret to releasing the resurrection power in them. Faith is the pipeline for the release of this power, the greater your faith, the greater the pipe through which the power flows, and the greater the power flowing, the greater the power released, and the greater the power released, the greater the results. I remember someone came and held my hand after a meeting that she wanted to receive a bit of power.

I do not have more power than you have, I might only have learned how to release the same power which is in all of us. Think of anybody who demonstrates power in their ministry. The simple fact is they have learned to provide a great channel for the flow and release of the resurrection power locked up in each one of us. You have untold power in the inside of you. Smith Wigglesworth said you are a thousand times bigger in the inside than you are on the outside. This is all because of the resurrection power He has placed in you. Step out and begin to use the power.

Proclaim what you are

Father, I thank you for what You say concerning me. I believe Your word with all my heart and. with all my soul. I refuse to believe what my circumstances say. I refuse to believe what people say. I stand on your word and therefore confess that I am what You say I am. And I am who You say I am.

Thank You for the power You have put in me, the same resurrection power that raised Jesus Christ from the dead. Lord by faith I will begin to use this power to set free captives and bring life to situations which appear hopeless. Lord I will release Your power in me by faith, to work in the lives of the oppressed, in Jesus' Name, amen.

93

THERE ARE RIVERS FLOWING INSIDE OF YOU

(John 7:37-38)

"In the last day, that great day of the feast, Jesus stood and cried saying, "If any man thirst, let him come unto me and drink. He that believeth on me, as the scripture hath said, out of his belly shall flow rivers of living water."

The Lord said, anyone who believes in Him shall have rivers of life-giving waters flowing from the inside of them. I want you to know that there are rivers of living water flowing in the inside of you. When that river level goes down, the amount of energy to light up your life also drops. You know the amount of hydroelectric power generated in any river depends on the volume of water that is flowing. The greater the volume of water, the greater the power which can be generated and vice versa.

To keep your light brightest you must ensure that the largest possible volume of water is flowing through you. This depends on your connection to the main source of your river – the Holy Spirit. As you allow the Holy Spirit to flow in you and through you, so are the rivers flowing to touch the lives of others. A river without the proper outlet soon becomes a lake and loses the *'life'* that is in it. The peculiarity of a river is that it sweeps away debris that falls in it. Your life can only be as clean as the volume of rivers flowing through you.

Open up your life and let the waters flow to give life to any dying thing around you. There is a river of living joy in you. There is a river of living love in you. There is a river of living hope in you. There is a river of living faith in you. There is a river of living peace in you. Let these rivers flow and bless the people around you. What you need to maintain a heavy flow in your life is the rain of the Spirit. Without His rain

Proclaim what you are

Father, I thank you for what You say concerning me. I believe Your word with all my heart and with all my soul. I refuse to believe what my circumstances say. I refuse to believe what people say. I stand on your word and therefore confess that I am what You say I am. And I am who You say I am.

Help me stay connected to Your Spirit so that the rivers will flow through me to others and never run dry. Lord, I open my life to the rain from above, to keep the rivers flowing high and strong, in Jesus' Name, amen.

# #
94

EVERYTHING IS POSSIBLE FOR YOU IF YOU BELIEVE

(Mark 9:23)

"If you can'?" said Jesus. "Everything is possible for him who believes."

This is not the general believing but faith expressed in a particular expectation to see it granted. It talks of the belief exercised and demonstrated when one desires a particular result to be produced. Because you have believed On the Lord Jesus, it is possible for you to believe Him for particular situations. The word impossible should not be part of your life and affaires. The extent of your belief is the extent of your results. The believer lives in a world of possibilities; where everything is possible and nothing is impossible. Why many of us don't see extraordinary results is because we do not believe God for extraordinary things.

If you want to see the impossible made possible, then you must believe God for impossible things. I realised I have been believing God only for the things which are possible. I am stepping out to believe Him for things which have heretofore not been possible in the history of mankind. I am reaching out for things which have not been possible in the history of my life. It is time for you to break records. If you have to break records then believe God for the *"unbelievable"* and walk the realms of impossibilities made possible by the power that is in the Name of Jesus Christ of Nazareth.

Proclaim what you are

Father, I thank you for what You say concerning me. I believe Your word with all my heart and with all my soul. I refuse to believe what my circumstances say. I refuse to believe what people say. I stand on your word and therefore confess that I am what You say I am. And I am who You say I am.

Lord, help me exercise my faith to believe You for the impossible. I want to stretch my faith to levels I have never done before. I am reaching out for more Lord, help me to walk the realms of impossibilities made possible, in Jesus' Name, amen.

95

GOD HAS MADE YOU INVINCIBLE

(Joshua 1:5)

"No one will be able to stand up against you all the days of your life. As I was with Moses, so I will be with you; I will never leave you nor forsake you."

God told Joshua that, *"As I was... so I will be"*. Ours is a God who never changes, from age to age He is the same in power, wisdom, authority etc. He told Joshua that no one would be able to stand up against him. It is the same promise He has for you. If you walk according to His precepts, then all your enemies are bound to fall before you because God has so decreed. From today I want you to live knowing that you cannot be defeated by the enemy. God has made you unbeatable and impregnable. The enemy will come but he will not be able to stand against you. He may even appear to make some progress in advancing against you but he will stumble before he reaches you.

I am amazed at the way the Lord has worked it out for me time and again when I thought the enemy was almost overcoming, then I just had the victory. Increasingly the fact that God has made me indomitable has given me confidence. Look at what He says, *"as I was... so I will be"*. You are serving the God of yesterday, today and forever. He is *"Jesus Christ the same, yesterday, today and forever"*. As He was with Moses, so will He be with you.

The Moses who could not be killed by the sword of pharaoh, or drowned in the River Nile, the Moses who could not be swallowed by years of suffering in the wilderness, the Moses who defeated kings and partitioned their kingdoms as an inheritance for the people of God; as God was with him, so will God be with you. That is His promise and you've got to believe it.

Proclaim what you are

Father, I thank you for what You say concerning me. I believe Your word with all my heart and with all my soul. I refuse to believe what my circumstances say. I refuse to believe what people say. I stand on your word and therefore confess that I am what You say I am. And I am who You say I am.

Thank you for your promise that no enemy will be bale to stand up against me all the days of my life. I will walk in your precepts and meditate on your word to build my confidence. I will face every battle knowing You have decreed victory for me, in Jesus' Name, amen.

96

YOU HAVE DIVINE IMMUNITY

(Psalm 105:15)

"Do not touch my anointed ones; do my prophets no harm."

God has granted you immunity from the hand of the evil one. When he says touch not, they are bound to obey, because it is an order from the King of the universe. You see the truth is that satan and his demons know this decree and they steer clear of believers. However, there are satanists who are ignorant and so the devil uses their ignorance to send them to danger zones. When they come, they obviously meet their doom.

I remember during one deliverance session when I realised the girl we were ministering deliverance to had been possessed by the high priestess of the marine kingdom to which she belonged. Of course, she came to resist and hinder the deliverance. When I realised this through a word of wisdom, I had to punish her very seriously, she left screaming after all the punishment I gave her. While the demon spirits had fled, she came to resist and received a taste of the power of the Holy Spirit. As long as you live the cross life, the devil can do you no harm. As long as you remain under the cover of the blood of the Lamb, everything respects the divine immunity upon your life.

Proclaim what you are

Father, I thank you for what You say concerning me. I believe Your word with all my heart and with all my soul. I refuse to believe what my circumstances say. I refuse to believe what people say. I stand on your word and therefore confess that I am what You say I am. And I am who You say I am.

Thank you for granting me immunity from all attacks of the evil one. I will remain under the cover of the cross and your blood. I will not break the hedge that surrounds me through sinful compromise, in Jesus' name, amen.

# #
97

YOUR DELIVERANCE IS GUARANTEED
(Psalm 34:19)

"A righteous man may have many troubles, but the LORD delivers him from them all"

The Lord did not promise that you will never find yourself in difficult situations. Many people easily give up in the face of adversity because they ceased to expect deliverance. Some could just wait thus far and when deliverance did not come when they thought it should, they rather gave up. Listen, I want to tell you that, no matter how difficult the situation that comes your way may be, God has promised you deliverance and so you can wait with all expectancy and assurance that though it tarry, it will surely come. It is not a matter of if it will come but one of when it will come. As long as you are a righteous, though your afflictions may be many, there will be deliverance from all of them.

You must live each day in anticipation of divine intervention in everything that concerns you which may appear to be going wrong. Never allow yourself to resign into the backdrop of defeat and despair. Never allow yourself to be relegated into the ravine of hopelessness. Hope is the lifeline of deliverance because hope is the ground on which faith is demonstrated. Now I want you to write down the things which are troubles to your life. Address each one and declare the fact that the Lord has delivered and will deliver you from all of them. Make it your routine until you see it manifested in the physical.

Proclaim what you are

Father, I thank you for what You say concerning me. I believe Your word with all my heart and with all my soul. I refuse to believe what my circumstances say. I refuse to believe what people say. I stand on your word and therefore confess that I am what You say I am. And I am who You say I am.

Thank You Lord because You have guaranteed deliverance from all my troubles. Whatever the trouble may me, I will face each day in anticipation of Your mighty deliverance, in Jesus' Name, amen.

# #
98

YOU SHOULD ALWAYS BE AT THE TOP

(Deuteronomy 28:13)

> *"The LORD will make you the head, not the tail. If you pay attention to the commands of the LORD your God that I give you this day and carefully follow them, you will always be at the top, never at the bottom."*

The Lord has given you the secret to excellence in whatever domain you are in. The principles of success remain the same no matter your sphere of business. If you walk according to divine precepts, then success is guaranteed for you. And it is not just any kind of success but that which catapults you to the top of your area of calling. So, any time you fine yourself at the bottom, know that you are in the wrong place. You are ordained to be at the top.

Permanent failure is not your portion; any failure that comes is to prepare you for unprecedented success that you otherwise would not be able to handle. The top is the place for you to stay. You have seen people rise from nowhere to the top. The simple reason is the discovery of divine principles for excellence. You serve a God of extraordinary excellence. You cannot afford to be a mediocre. Mediocrity is a foreign attribute to any child of God because the genes in you are genes of the God of all excellence. He does well whatever He does and that same capacity is locked up in the inside of you. Refuse the bottom line Christianity. Resist the draw of mediocrity and soar to the heights ordained for you by the Lord.

Proclaim what you are

Father, I thank you for what You say concerning me. I believe Your word with all my heart and with all my soul. I refuse to believe what my circumstances say. I refuse to believe what people say. I stand on your word and therefore confess that I am what You say I am. And I am who You say I am.

Lord I reject mediocrity and go for excellence. I will put in my all and tap into Your revealed principles for success. Help me apply the principles of success and excellence as revealed in Your word, in Jesus' Name, amen.

# #
99

GOD KNOWS WHAT YOU NEED

(Matthew 6:8; Philippians 4:19)

"Do not be like them, for your Father knows what you need before you ask him."
"And my God will meet all your needs according to his glorious riches in Christ Jesus."

All that you need, both the ones you are aware of and those you are unaware of are known by your Father even before you ask Him to provide. All you have to do is present your needs as simply as you can without trying to get God to understand you. He has promised that He will meet all your needs according to His riches. Those silent needs in your heart are known by Him. However, He has ordained that you ask in order to receive. He is committed to meet all your needs more than you ever think, but by divine principles you will have to ask.

He says even before you call He will answer, but it is the call that releases the answer which has already been provided. The call is like the switch that releases the current to flow to the device. That is what your asking does; it releases that which has already been provided to come to you. You are not dealing with an unwilling God, the God you serve is more than willing and ready to meet every need of yours as you reach out to Him in prayer, expectation and faith.

Proclaim what you are

Father, I thank you for what You say concerning me. I believe Your word with all my heart and with all my soul. I refuse to believe what my circumstances say. I refuse to believe what people say. I stand on your word and therefore confess that I am what You say I am. And I am who You say I am.

Thank you Lord, because You know my every need. I refuse to worry and be anxious about any thing but through prayer I will make my needs known to You and by faith receive what I ask for, in Jesus' Name, amen.

# #
100

YOU ARE USELESS WITHOUT CHRIST JESUS

(John 15:5)

"I am the vine; you are the branches. If a man remains in me and I in him, he will bear much fruit; apart from me you can do nothing."

Now, all what has been said here depends on your understanding of this point. Though I placed it towards the end it is most important of all the things which God has said about you because, unless it is understood, you may be deceived to think that it is because you are better than others that's why such things have been said of you. If there is only one thing you should get from this book, then it should be this point; that without Christ you are nothing, you can do nothing, and you can become nothing of worth in the sight of God.

You are what you are today because of Christ. You must acknowledge it always so that you will not begin looking at yourself. Let your gaze be continually on the Lord, confess the fact that you are nothing without Him and live to depend on Him always. He is your source, anchor, hope, joy and everything. Daily acknowledge the fact that all that you are or could ever be is because of Him. That is why throughout scripture, especially in the epistles, you will often find the phrase, *"in him"*.

Proclaim what you are

Father, I thank you for what You say concerning me. I believe Your word with all my heart and with all my soul. I refuse to believe what my circumstances say. I refuse to believe what people say. I stand on your word and therefore confess that I am what You say I am. And I am who You say I am.

Lord, it is in Christ Jesus, that all what You have said about me counts. Help me to live daily in him and for Him so that all what You have said concerning will become part of my daily experience, in Jesus' Name, amen.

# #
101

IT SHALL BE WELL WITH YOU

(Isaiah 3:10a)

"Tell the righteous it will be well with them…"

That is an announcement from the Throne of grace that should set you shouting out for victory. God says to tell you that all will be well with you. It does not matter what your past experiences have been. It does not matter what appears to be happening now in the physical. But the Lord says, He is arranging everything for your well being.

It shall be well with your finances
It shall be well with your business
It shall be well with your job
It shall be well with your marriage
It shall be well with your academics
It shall be well with your ministry.

That is what heaven says to announce to you. And as long as heaven says it then we can trust that it will be just as He has promised. Do not focus on the circumstances but on what He has said in His unfailing word concerning you. It shall be well with you, if you believe it and declare it in accordance with what God has already said, it will surely come to pass. Do you remember the woman at Shumen? When her son died and she went to the prophet, she told her husband, *"it shall be well"*. When she got to the man of God and was asked what the matter was, she said, *"it is well"*.

That is the kind of faith you must confess daily. God has said it will be well with you, so will it be. You have the responsibility to proclaim it to every situation which may want to go the contrary.

Proclaim what you are

Father, I thank you for what You say concerning me. I believe Your word with all my heart and with all my soul. I refuse to believe what my circumstances say. I refuse to believe what people say. I stand on your word and therefore confess that I am what You say I am. And I am who You say I am.

I confess that it will be well with me in every aspect of my life. I refuse to believe what the circumstances are saying. You have said it will be well with me, Lord I believe it and will proclaim it daily, in Jesus' name, amen.

# #
102

YOU WILL ENJOY THE FRUIT OF YOUR LABOUR

(Isaiah 3:10b)

"... For they shall enjoy the fruit of their deeds"

The time for fruitless labour for you is past! From this day henceforth you will enjoy the fruit of all your labour. The devil shall not steal your harvest any more.

You will enjoy the fruit of your prayers
You will enjoy the fruit of your fasts
You will enjoy the fruit of your giving
You will enjoy the fruit of your evangelism
You will enjoy the fruit of your studies
You will enjoy the fruit of your marriage
You will enjoy the fruit of your sacrifices
You will enjoy the fruit of your hard work
You will enjoy the fruit of your investments.

That is heaven's declaration concerning you. From today you shall not allow the devil to cheat you of your blessings. Fruitless labour is not your portion! Is there any where you have laboured and it seems the fruits are not forth coming? Address it with the word of God. Refuse to be cheated by circumstances set in motion by the enemy. What God has said must be obeyed by all creation. You have the commission to reinforce divine decrees and announcements.

Proclaim what you are

Father, I thank you for what You say concerning me. I believe Your word with all my heart and with all my soul. I refuse to believe what my circumstances say. I refuse to believe what people say. I stand on your word and therefore confess that I am what You say I am. And I am who You say I am.

Lord I will not give up labouring for fear that I won't enjoy the fruits of my labour. Lord I call forth the fruits now in all the places and areas I have laboured, in the Name of Jesus' amen.

# #
103

Your life is hidden with Christ in God

(Colossians 3:3)

"For you died, and your life is now hidden with Christ in God"

That which has been hidden by God cannot be uncovered by the enemy. God has hidden your life with Christ Jesus in Himself. That means you are beyond the reach of the enemy. If Christ cannot be touched because of where He is then you too cannot be touched because the same place Christ is that is where you have been hidden. It is very comforting to know you are in a special place in God.

Your dwelling place is God Himself. That is what the Bible says. So, from today begin to see yourself as beyond the reach of the enemy. Isn't it amazing that the Lord will do such a thing for you? The verse above is not a possibility. Paul says it's an accomplished fact. It has nothing to do with you, God did it on His own. You cannot be touched by the enemy. God has to grant him access into Himself, then a second access into Christ, then a third access to you. Your life is hid with Christ in God, hallelujah!

Proclaim what you are

Father, I thank you for what You say concerning me. I believe Your word with all my heart and with all my soul. I refuse to believe what my circumstances say. I refuse to believe what people say.

I stand on your word and therefore confess that I am what You say I am. And I am who You say I am.

I am glad that my life is hid with Christ in You, oh God. Thank you for the security I have in You. I will live for You in confidence and boldness each and everyday, in Jesus' Name, amen.

104

YOU ARE MARRIED TO CHRIST

(Romans 7:2; 2Corinthians 11:2)

With the increase phenomena of spirit wives and husbands, it is but necessary that you know your position in Christ. You have been betrothed to Christ. You are part of His Bride. This means any spirit husband or wife is operating on an illegal basis. If you see signs of your life being tormented because of ties to a spirit spouse, on the basis of your everlasting marriage to Jesus, rebuke the demon and judge all of his or her operations in your life because your Husband lives forever more. If you are in Christ, even if such a relationship with a spirit spouse had been pre-established, you have the mandate to renounce it because your position in Christ sets you free from any inferior covenant with the enemy.

Proclaim what you are

Father, I thank you for what You say concerning me. I believe Your word with all my heart and with all my soul. I refuse to believe what my circumstances say. I refuse to believe what people say. I stand on your word and therefore confess that I am what You say I am. And I am who You say I am.

I reject and renounce every marriage covenant made on my behalf or by myself whether knowingly or unknowingly. I have but one husband who is Jesus Christ. I belong to Christ Jesus with my whole spirit, soul, and body, in Jesus' name, amen.

# #
105

GOD WILL GIVE YOU SINGLENESS OF HEART

(Jeremiah 32:39)

"I will give them singleness of heart and action, so that they will always fear me and that all will then go well for them and for their children after them."

If there is one problem with many believers, it is dividedness of heart. And with such a heart condition there is no way you can perform at your best. God knows that you cannot enter into your full inheritance if you operate with a double heart and so He has promised to give you singleness of heart and action. That is, He wants to make you in such a way that all your actions will agree with what originates from your own very heart. It is your place to appropriate this gift and be at your best for the Lord. Singleness of heart and action is a virtue to be desired and sought. There is nothing as useless as a divided heart, but this seems to be one of the greatest ills that have plagued human kind. Ask the Lord for a single heart and believe that He has given you.

Proclaim what you are

Father, I thank you for what You say concerning me. I believe Your word with all my heart and with all my soul. I refuse to believe what my circumstances say. I refuse to believe what people say.

I stand on your word and therefore confess that I am what You say I am. And I am who You say I am.

Lord, I ask from You a single heart, I receive it by faith, in Jesus' Name, amen.

CONCLUSION

We said before that knowledge is power. What you know will affect what you do and what you eventually become. The purpose of this book is that by knowing what God says about you, you can take sides with God by confessing and declaring the things He has said about you. In declaring them you should also ensure that you live according to the precepts and principles of life revealed in the word of God. Confessing without complying will produce no result. It is as you comply with what God says that your prayers and confession of what He has said about you will produce the required results. So from today onward, because you now know, you should become what God says you should become

Other publications from the publisher

Other publications from the publisher

Other publications from the publisher

Other publications from the publisher

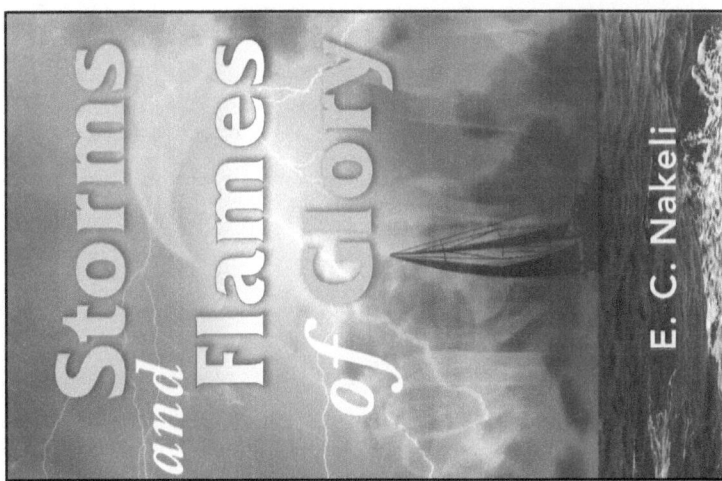

www.ingramcontent.com/pod-product-compliance
Lightning Source LLC
Chambersburg PA
CBHW021144080526
44588CB00008B/212